BERLITZ®

KU-613-187

PARIS

- A ✔ in the text denotes a highly recommended sight
- A complete A–Z of practical information starts on p.115
- Extensive mapping throughout: on cover flaps and in text

2nd Edition (1995/1996)

**Although we make every effort to ensure the accuracy of the
information in this guide, changes do occur. If you have any new
information, suggestions or corrections to contribute, we would like
to hear from you. Please write to Berlitz Publishing at the above
address.**

Text:	Giles Allen
Photography:	Claude Huber, except those on pages 32 (top)
	and 44 by Monique Jacot;
	pages 60 and 104 by Erling Mandelmann;
	and page 86 by kind permission of the Louvre.
Cartography:	🚂 Falk-Verlag, Hamburg

We wish to thank the Office de Tourisme de Paris for
their help in the preparation of this guide.

CONTENTS

Paris and the Parisians

'*A nous deux, Paris.*' ('It's between the two of us now, Paris.') Balzac's Rastignac said it, but we all feel it. That rising exhilaration as we arrive seizes us all, whether on a first visit or a twenty-first. Something about the city makes us come to life, and though the faint-hearted may find the pace daunting at first, soon the magic will take over.

Whatever your interests, moods and temperament, there is a Paris for you – there is a Paris for everyone. From the scholarly, happiest browsing through books along the *bouquinistes* by the Seine, to the rugby supporter cheering on the opposing team at the Parc des Princes, everyone to his or her Paris. *You* choose.

Why then is Paris so demanding? Because it's a city that asks you to participate; to join in the search for quality, beauty, style and fun. The Parisians are hedonists – they go for the best in everything, armed with an apparently invincible self-confidence. Look around you: from the gardens, buildings and monuments to the shops, the food and the people, style is all.

Take a seat at the terrace of a café and watch the world go by, at its pace or yours. Café terraces are the best bargain in Paris, even if your drink costs you a little more than at the counter. Every passer-by is putting on a wonderful performance, vying for attention with the greatest aplomb. Or study your fellow diners. Watch the mobility of their faces, switching rapidly from one mood to the next. Confidence, it seems, is the keystone to Paris and its people. If it spills over into arrogance on occasions, you'll nevertheless have to admit that it achieves marvels. Every stone and monument, from the Champs-Elysées to the Pyramide du Louvre, bear witness to the Parisians' inherent belief that their city is best.

But Paris isn't just about people and buildings – nature **5** seems to have wanted to play its part, too. Where else would you find such beautiful light? Each season holds its own particular charm. A Parisian winter is nothing to dread; indeed, certain monuments are at their best under the cold, crisp light. The autumn, when leaves turn from gold to brown, holds almost as much romance as spring, when the gardens come to life and an all-pervading sense of joy fills the air. Summer is when the city really comes into its own, and if it's deserted by Parisians in August, the traffic is at least manageable and the people that remain take time to relax. And when night falls, Paris offers unparalleled illumination of its major historic buildings, avenues and squares.

While many commuters trek in from the suburbs to work, chased from the capital by high rents and lack of suitable accommodation, a lot of people still live in the city, making Paris one of the most densely populated urban areas in the world. The city is constantly on the move; day and night, throngs take to the streets, cafés and pavements.

Paris today is a giant work site; the city is forever being chiselled and polished. Of course, there's the reverse side of the coin: the dejected *clochards* begging in metros and living in cardboard boxes, and the poorer families, evicted *de facto* from their Paris homes and hounded out to soulless suburbs.

It's a commonplace to say that Paris has changed almost out of recognition since the heady days of May 1968, when the Establishment was shaken to the core. The young revolutionaries have become the Establishment in their turn, but tradition has never been the same again. The wind of change that swept through the capital brought with it new goals and aspirations. Paris yearned to be modern. It was determined to be the indisputable capital of the arts. And it succeeded.

It started with President Pompidou, who laid down the *voie expresse* along the river bank, the foundations of the Défense complex and the Centre Pompidou (Beaubourg); it continued with Giscard d'Estaing's Musée d'Orsay and Chirac's Centre Omnisports de Paris-Bercy; and reached its peak with Mitterrand's Pyramide du Louvre, Cité des Sciences et de l'Industrie at La Villette, the Grande Arche de la Défense, not to mention the perhaps less successful Ministère de l'Economie et des Finances, the Opéra-Bastille, the Arab Institute, and the TGB (Très Grande Bibliothèque or Very Large Library) now at last underway. And then there are the just-outside-Paris attractions, like the new Euro Disneyland complex.

However, buildings don't tell the whole story. The countless new '*salons*' (or international fairs), museums and shows, and the constant improvements to its already good communications system make Paris a pole of attraction – and one that is constantly growing.

President Mitterrand, when he launched his vast building programme in 1981, took the view that the state had an important role to play in the urban development of the capital. Why? Because a city is always subject to external forces which, if left to themselves, would impart a disorderly stamp on the cityscape, and it is up to the state to act as an arbiter and to see that urban harmony is maintained.

This is nothing new – from the formal Tuileries Gardens set out by André Le Nôtre in 1664 for Louis XIV, to President Pompidou's Beaubourg, order imposed by 'decision makers' has given Paris a disciplined, even severe look.

Brusque, rude, hostile, the Parisian? Scarcely. The sometimes gruff exterior conceals a sensitive soul, caustic for sure, but alert and ready to engage in countless battles of wits, in a country where to be articulate is as inbred as understanding the secrets of cuisine.

To call a person an intellectual in France is still a compliment, and discussions or analysis of a wide-ranging list of subjects – from politics and philosophy to art and social issues – provide the mainstay of many a café conversation. A trifle inclined to jeer, perhaps? No doubt, but if that helps clear the daily moroseness, why not?

Who is 'the Parisian', anyway? Only one in two is actually born there. Most hail from the provinces, from Brittany or Burgundy, from Corsica or Corrèze – adding different ingredients to the Paris 'stew' – and within a few years they are Parisian through and through, showing contempt for 'provincials' (who return the com-pliment), while remaining fiercely loyal, when talking to foreigners or their grandchildren, to the province they left. And today the immigrant population from the Maghreb and Africa, as well as from France's overseas' *départements*, have added a colourful ingredient to the mix. If problems of integration sometimes come to the surface, time is gradually allaying them.

After years of indifferent performances, Paris's opera, ballet and theatre have recently achieved worldwide acclaim. Musicians, singers, tennis players – every star in every discipline wants to appear in Paris. The French film

Visitors gather round the colourful Stravinsky Fountain at the Centre Pompidou.

industry may be in the doldrums, but it still leads the way in Europe. Art exhibitions bring crowds flocking from all over France and Europe, and the Japanese can't keep away. The Musée d'Orsay recorded 4 million visitors in its first year, the Louvre records 3 million visitors a year, and even the Business Centre of La Défense (thanks mostly to the Grande Arche) is taken by storm daily. The new attractions have started to rival the old.

If Paris is a melting pot of people and cultures, it has,

strangely enough, no cuisine it can call its own – which doesn't matter because it harbours the best of all the regional cuisines. And if you tire of French food or, more likely, have a surfeit of it, you'll find an endless list of first-rate international restaurants to choose from.

The Left Bank still looks askance at the Right, distinct in mentality despite a gradual fudging at the seams. Virtually all the publishing houses and many art galleries and bookshops lie on the Rive Gauche, the intellectuals' bank, while the Right has always attracted the Establishment: the big names in fashion and cuisine, banks, offices and grand hotels. But it isn't that simple. Since in general French hearts lie on the Left and their wallets on the Right, many have a foot in both camps. Therefore, galleries or *grandes maisons* have branches on both the Left and Right Banks to cater to their respective clienteles. If for decades after the War the young made a beeline for the 'intellectual' Left Bank, leaving the Right to 'philistine' businessmen, today the pendulum has swung back, and the evenings are as lively in the newly transformed Halles and Beaubourg areas or around the Bastille and its new Opera as in the traditional cafés of Saint-Germain.

The Luxembourg Gardens provide the perfect setting for a spot of sunbathing.

11

Like most big cities, Paris evolves within its defined perimeters. There are 20 *arondissements*, or districts, each with its own specific character. Ethnic groups lend an exotic blast of colour to one street, while the next holds fashionable, discreet *fin-de-siècle* flats and a stately avenue spawns a tangle of little streets. Former working-class areas have become the height of chic, while some chic areas have slid into decline. And behind the classic or well-trodden tourist paths, you'll find delightful streets, ideal for a stroll and a peek behind the *portes cochères* (carriage entrances), where you'll catch a glimpse of peaceful courtyards and pretty façades.

Watch life, window shop or wander aimlessly – an activity perfectly summed up in the verb *flâner*. You'll find that the famous slogan takes on a truth for the whole city: 'there is always something happening'. Balzac didn't have to go far to look for his *comédie humaine* – it lay at his doorstep.

The powers of attraction Paris wields are such, the magic spell it casts so strong, that few visitors leave the city indifferent. It will adopt you if you adopt it – just join in and take part in the action. Hundreds and thousands of visitors, from all corners of the earth, have succumbed, have been adopted or are being adopted. And it would be strange indeed if you didn't feel you were. Subtly, without even noticing it ... you've become a Parisian, too.

A Brief History

Defence

Defence came first, beauty simply followed. The choice of Paris, or Lutetia (marshland) as its original inhabitants, the Parisii, called it, was brilliant. In the middle of the swift-flowing River Seine, far wider then than it is today, the Celtic fishermen set up their homes on an island, the present Ile de la Cité. It provided first-rate protection against most invaders, but not against the Romans, who conquered the town in 52 BC.

In Roman times, the Right Bank of the river was too marshy to live on, so the town expanded to the Left Bank. In their customary fashion, the Romans endowed it with temples, straight roads, markets and trustworthy bridges. Excavation work has revealed the Roman arena – popular for fights between gladiators, lions and Christians – and the public baths (see p.58), dating from the 2nd and 3rd centuries AD.

St Denis brought Christianity to the city and was rewarded by decapitation on the hill of Montmartre in around 250 AD. Legend and popular depictions of the event have Denis picking up his head and walking away with it.

Towards the end of the 3rd century Lutetia, which had taken on the name of Paris round about this time, was overrun by barbarians, mostly Huns and Franks, and the town's inhabitants moved back to the fortified Ile de la Cité. Attila headed this way in 451, but the fervour of St Geneviève's prayers is said to have persuaded him to spare the city. A shepherdess who abandoned her flocks in the present-day suburb of Nanterre, she died, venerated by all, at a ripe old age in 502. Clovis, King of the Franks, who showed good faith by converting to Christianity, arrived in 486 and settled down in the Palais de la Cité (now Palais de Justice). People moved back to the Left Bank, and the church of Saint-Germain-des-Prés was built in the 6th century.

A Capital is Born

Though technically the country's main town, Paris wasn't sufficiently armed or organized to fight off the Normans who, from 861, plundered it at regular intervals. It remained a quiet backwater on the European scene until Hugues Capet established himself there in 987 and made Paris the economic and political capital of France for the Capetian dynasty. Under Louis VI (1108–37) Paris enjoyed its 'agricultural age', when enclosed farms, or *clos*, flourished. But the strength of Paris lay in its merchants, who exploited the commerce of the Seine by collecting taxes and duties from the ships passing through the capital, making the town rich under the motto: *Fluctuat nec mergitur* (It floats but doesn't sink). This explains the ship on Paris's flag. The port area, known as the *Grève*, developed on the Right Bank by the present-day Châtelet and Hôtel de Ville.

These revenues enabled Philippe Auguste (1180–1223) to build the cathedral of Notre-Dame, a fortress named the Louvre and some aqueducts, and to install fresh-water fountains and some paved streets. The town had 36 streets in the *Cité*, 80 in the *Université* (Left Bank) and 194 on the Right

The Arc de Triomphe is the crowning glory of the Champs-Elysées. Below: a detail of La Marseillaise, *by François Rude.*

Bank. To protect his investment while away on the Third Crusade (1189–1192), Philippe Auguste surrounded the growing city with walls.

Louis IX (1226–70) developed the spiritual and intellectual side of Paris life by building the Gothic masterpiece, the Sainte-Chapelle, and many colleges on the Left Bank, including that of Robert de Sorbon in 1257 (see p.57). At the end of his reign, and with a population of 100,000, Paris had become the largest and most magnificent city in Western Christendom, and a pole of attraction for the rest of Europe.

The mercantile backbone of the city proved itself in the 14th century, when the plague and the Hundred Years' War devastated the country, leaving Paris at the mercy of the English. In 1356, with King Jean le Bon taken prisoner at Poitiers, the provost of the city merchants, Etienne Marcel,

took advantage of the confusion and set up a municipal dictatorship. Though assassinated a year later, Marcel had shown that the Parisians themselves were a force to be reckoned with in France's history. The next king, Charles V, ever wary of Parisian militancy, built the Bastille fortress.

If the strife of the 14th century had been unsettling for Paris, that of the 15th was positively disastrous. In 1407, the Duke of Burgundy had the Duke of Orleans murdered on the Rue Barbette, which led to 12 years of strife between the Burgundians and the Armagnacs. The carnage ended only with the capture of Paris by the English in 1420. Ten years later, Joan of Arc tried and failed to liberate the town, and a year later came the ultimate humiliation: the young English King Henry VI was

The Hôtel de Ville, built under François I, burnt to the ground during the Commune and was completely rebuilt in 1873.

crowned King of France at Notre-Dame Cathedral. As if that wasn't enough, the plague of 1466 felled thousands of Parisians.

Pride without Prejudice

And yet Paris held up under it all. With François I (1515–47), the city learned to thrive under an absolutist and absentee monarch, busy with wars in Italy and even a year's imprisonment in Spain. The arts, sciences and literature flourished. Much of the Louvre was torn down and rebuilt along the present lines. A new Hôtel de Ville (town hall) was begun, as well as the superb Saint-Eustache church. The Parisians were already assuming that distinctive pride over the uniqueness of their town. Villon sang: '*Il n'y a bon bec que de Paris*' (only Parisians have real wit), while the poet Pierre de Ronsard saw Paris as 'the city imbued with the discipline and glory of the muses'.

The bloody religious wars wreaked havoc and mayhem **17**

in Paris, starting in 1572 with the infamous Massacre of St Bartholomew – 3,000 Protestants were killed – and culminating in the siege of the city by Henri de Navarre in 1589. Before the Catholic League capitulated, 13,000 Parisians had died of starvation. Henri was crowned at Chartres and finally entered the city in 1594 – but not before he had turned Catholic. His famous words, 'Paris is well worth a mass', have remained an ambiguous comment on the merely political value attached to religion and the special desirability of the French capital. Paris's myth was growing.

Henri IV did Paris proud once he was its master. He built the beautiful Place des Vosges and Place Dauphine, embellished the river banks with the Quais de l'Arsenal, de l'Horloge and des Orfèvres, and constructed the Samaritaine hydraulic machine that pumped fresh water to the Right Bank households up until 1813. By far the most popular of France's monarchs,

'le bon roi Henri' was a notorious ladies' man and was known to his subjects as the Vert Galant. He completed the Pont-Neuf (new then, but today the oldest standing bridge in Paris) and the adjacent gardens, where he had been known to dally with his ladies.

Under Louis XIII (1610–43), Paris began to take on the 'fashionable' aspect that has become its hallmark. The Cours-la-Reine, precursor of the Champs-Elysées, was built for Henri's widow, Marie de Médicis. Elegant houses went up along the Faubourg Saint-Honoré, superb *hôtels* mushroomed in the Marais area, and tree-lined boulevards stretched clear across the city over to the Bastille, creating the airy sweep of modern Paris. The capital also consolidated its position as the hub of the country, with the establish-

The Palais-Bourbon's classical façade harbours the Assemblée Nationale, seat of the French Parliament.

ment of the royal printing press, Cardinal Richelieu's Académie Française and other scientific institutions (such as the botanical gardens), and the capital's new ecclesiastical status as an archbishopric. The cardinal also deserves credit for the splendid Palais-Royal. The Ile Saint-Louis, formed from two separate islands in 1614 by the engineer Christophe Marie, and the residential development of the Marais and the Saint-Germain-des-Prés districts made Paris an increasingly attractive place for nobles from the provinces.

Too much so for the liking of King Louis XIV (1643–1715). To bring his overly powerful and independent aristocrats back into line, he decided to move the court to Versailles, a stone's throw from the capital, where palace life was ruinously expensive. Paris became a political backwater, but continued to flourish with the landscaping (by

Jean-Baptiste Colbert, Louis' councellor) of the Tuileries Gardens and the Champs-Elysées, the construction of the Louvre's great colonnade, the triumphal arches of Saint-Antoine, Saint-Denis and Saint-Martin and the Invalides hospital for wounded soldiers. The Sun-King's wariness of the Parisian talent for trouble-making led to the innovation of street-lighting (on moonless nights only). The city now numbered 560,000 inhabitants, almost six times as many as in the 13th century.

Paris asserted its cultural ascendancy in Europe with the organization of the academies of the arts, literature and sciences and the founding of the Comédie-Française (1680) and other theatres under Louis XV. Cafés sprang up around the Palais-Royal, and the boulevards became the animated focus of European intellectuals as the Revolution approached.

One of the last constructions of the Ancien Régime was a new 23km (14-mile) wall around the city. Begun in 1784, the wall became a major

The Pont Alexandre III provides the best vantage point over the graceful Hôtel des Invalides, Napoleon's last resting place.

factor in the unrest, for it was along it that the *fermiers-généraux* (financiers) collected taxes from merchants coming to do business in Paris.

Napoleon's Paris

The Revolution of 1789 was more notable for its destructions than for its additions to Parisian landmarks – though the removal of the Bastille and monasteries and convents did create more open spaces. The revolutionaries made special use of the stronghold of the Capetian dynasty: the Conciergerie in the Palais de Justice, the heart of the medieval kings' palace, became a prison for those condemned by Revolutionary tribunals. And Dr Joseph Guillotin, a member of parliament who said that times

20

demanded something more humane than the Ancien Régime's hanging, drawing and quartering, developed a new gadget to chop heads off.

With the advent of Napoleon, the city's development resumed. The Emperor's frequent absences on foreign business did not hinder his projects for making Paris the capital of Europe. Detailed maps of the city and architectural plans for new buildings never left his side. He even found time during his stopover in Moscow to work on the complete reorganization of the Comédie-Française back home. While most visitors see Napoleon's mark in spectacular monuments – the Arc de Triomphe, the 12 avenues off the Etoile and the column of the Grande-Armée on the Place Vendôme – the Emperor himself held his most important achievements to be his civic improvements, more appropriate to a mayor than a world conqueror: fresh water in quantity throughout the city, improved drainage, new food markets, five slaughter houses and the wine market. His streamlined municipal **21** administration and police force became a model for modern European urban government. He erected bridges over the Seine, started building the Stock Exchange, put up the church of the Madeleine in a Paris that then numbered 700,000 inhabitants and more than 1,000 streets.

The centralization of power in the capital also made Paris a potential threat to the government, with the concentration of aggressively ambitious bourgeois, dissatisfied workers and an intellectual class eager to try out its radical ideas. Typically, the Revolution of 1830 came from an alliance of liberal bourgeois Parisian intellectuals, denied the right to publish their newspapers, and the printing workers thrown into unemployment by the closing down of the papers. The 1848 Revolution which ended Louis-Philippe's 'bourgeois' monarchy also originated in Paris. Building up Paris as a great capital of cultural, social and political innovation automatically turned it into a **22** hotbed of trouble for its rulers.

Capital Facelift

Napoleon III, the great one's nephew, was literally scared into modernizing Paris. He had seen the popular uprisings of 1830 and 1848 flare up in the capital's densely populated working-class neighbourhoods around the city centre and wanted to prevent a recurrence. He therefore commissioned Baron Georges Haussmann to do away with the clusters of narrow streets and alleyways that nurtured discontent and barricades. The baron razed them and moved the occupants out to the suburbs, creating the 'red belt' which makes Paris one of the few Western capitals whose suburbs are not predominantly conservative. This ruthless approach made way for a 'new' Paris, far removed from the old in looks and spirit, but not without its own charm, too.

The city was opened up by wide boulevards and avenues, giving Paris its modern, airy look and highlighting the city's monumental churches and other public buildings. Furthermore, as the baron explained to his emperor, these avenues gave the artillery a clear line of fire in case of revolt. But this Second Empire was also a time of joyous abandon and boisterous expansion. World fairs in 1855 and 1867 attracted royalty from England, Austria, Russia and Prussia, eager to look at the sparkling new city portrayed in Offenbach's operettas and the comedies of Labiche. This was the beginning of 'gay Paree'.

Then came the Franco-Prussian War, with a crippling siege of Paris in 1870 and another uprising. The Paris Commune (self-government of the workers) lasted 10 weeks, from 18 March to 29 May 1871, until Adolphe Thiers, first president of the Third Republic, sent in troops from Versailles to crush the revolt.

Out – and Up

The Third Republic brought unparalleled prosperity to Paris. Projects begun under Napoleon III, such as the new opera house and the gigantic Halles market (today transferred to Rungis in the suburbs) were completed. The capital's triumphant resurrection after its defeat by the Prussians was marked by a construction boom. Star of the show was the Eiffel Tower (built in 1889), as techniques using iron improved out of recognition. Meanwhile, underground, the splendid new *métro* provided a rapid and comfortable means of transport through the city.

By the 1890s Paris had risen to the fore as a cultural magnet. Artists, writers and revolutionaries flocked to this hub of creative activity. The great Picasso arrived from Barcelona in 1900, followed by Modigliani from Livorno, Soutine from Minsk, Stravinsky from St Petersburg and Gertrude Stein from San Francisco. Then followed the long stream of American artists and writers led by Ernest Hemingway and F. Scott Fitzgerald.

Two wars, of course, took their toll. Though the Germans did not make it to Paris during **23** the First World War, they occupied the city for four drab years (June 1940 to August 1944) in the Second. Typically, what the French remember is the August parade of General de Gaulle and his fellow Resistance fighters down the Champs-Elysées; the expatriates' fondest memory, on the other hand, is of Ernest Hemingway 'liberating' the bar of the Ritz Hotel. Though at this point some of the cultural magnetism had moved from Paris to New York, the French capital still retained an element of its former cachet, with Jean-Paul Sartre holding court on the Left Bank and Juliette Greco singing in the jazz cellars of Saint-Germain-des-Prés.

In May 1968 students and workers recaptured some of the old revolutionary spirit. Walls were daubed with slogans as witty and pithy as ever and the Latin Quarter's paving stones were hurled at the smugly entrenched Establishment of de Gaulle's Fifth Republic. President Georges Pompidou picked up the pieces and affirmed the new prosperity with riverside expressways and skyscrapers, but his crowning achievement was the once controversial but now hugely successful Beaubourg Cultural Centre.

In 1977 Jacques Chirac became the first democratically elected mayor of Paris. (For over a century, since the turbulent days of the Commune, the national government controlled the city with its own appointed officials.) Now, in a country where politicians can double as mayor and prime minister, Parisians benefit from leaders eager to further their national political ambitions with a dynamic municipal performance: cleaner streets, sports facilities and improved traffic conditions.

President Mitterrand has made his own mark on Paris's skyline with a series of innovative, controversial but always impressive works: the Grande Arche, the Opéra-Bastille, the Institut du Monde Arabe, the Ministère des Finances and a whole project to reorganize the Louvre around a monumental glass pyramid.

Paris emerges the clear winner from this political one-upmanship. It has reasserted its domination in the creative arts, built model museums to display its fantastic heritage and continues to wield an astonishing cultural influence throughout the world.

The Grande Arche of La Défense (right) and the Ministère des Finances (below) proclaim Paris's faith in its future.

Where to Go

Getting About

Most travellers agree that Paris is one of the easiest big cities to get about. Traffic jams haven't gone away (they've got worse), but Paris has dared to face the future and built an efficient metro system that is smooth, rapid, regular and on time. Buses provide a pleasant alternative and also manage to give you a sightseeing tour at an exceptionally reasonable cost, while respecting, within reason, their schedules. Taxis provide a lazy alternative and remain affordable.

However, distances are not great and the majority of hotels in the 20 *arrondissements* are within walking distance of most sights. If time isn't a major factor, consider walking as a great option for getting the feel of the place. All you need is a stout, comfortable pair of shoes. Metro stations display excellent maps to help you use the network – a good reference for walkers, too. And more

and more places are being turned into pedestrian zones: parks, squares and gardens but also streets and whole areas, such as Beaubourg (Centre Pompidou) and Les Halles.

Picture the centre of Paris as a circle, with the river Seine acting as a thread down the middle of the city, stitching together many of the key *arrondissements*. Follow the riverbed and you are bound to come across a major point in the city, like the Place de la Concorde or the Louvre. Between the Gare de Lyon and the Boulevard de Grenelle, 27 bridges of all shapes and sizes criss-cross the river, binding the two banks together.

Look out for street numbers, too. Napoleon, in his wisdom, numbered all streets with even numbers on the right and odd numbers on the left. He headed from the Seine 'inland', and streets parallel to the river are numbered in an upstream-downstream direction.

Where to start? It's all too easy to be put off a place by setting off on the wrong foot so, if it's your first visit, why not take the *bateau mouche*? The guided boat trip will serve a double function: it will show you Paris under its most romantic light, and will also help you get an overall picture of the capital (see p.117).

For convenience, this book groups the major museums (or their contents at least) in a special section. Paris is home to countless museums and you will be faced with some difficult choices. A Museum Pass (see p.132) represents quite a bargain if you intend to do some serious museum-going.

It's a toss-up between the Right or Left Banks so, as a compromise, we start on the islands. Smack in the heart of Paris, they are convenient to get to and from and offer an excellent introduction to the capital: Paris and its river, inextricably linked, are never closer than on the sister isles. **27**

From the top of the Arc de Triomphe, look down on Paris's glorious avenues.

The Islands

ILE DE LA CITÉ

Fittingly enough for the cradle of a town that grew from its river trade, the Ile de la Cité is shaped like a boat, with the Square du Vert-Galant as its prow lunging out into the river. Here the original Parisii fishermen and bargees set up their dwellings, and through the centuries the pocket-sized island has remained the heart of the town.

The island also exemplifies what over-ambitious, wilful urban planning can do to charming neighbourhoods. In the middle of the 19th century, the much-praised but often heavy-handed Baron Haussmann swept away nearly all of the medieval and 17th-century structures, leaving only the Place Dauphine and the Rue Chanoinesse (ancient home of the cathedral canons) as evidence of the island's rich residential life.

The baron was also toying with the idea of replacing the triangular Place Dauphine's gracious red-brick architecture with a neo-Grecian colonnaded square when, luckily, he was forced out of office for juggling the books. This *place*, close by the lively Pont-Neuf, was built in 1607 by Henri IV in honour of his son the *dauphin* (later Louis XIII). Sadly, only the houses at numbers 14 and 26 are still in their original state, since 18th-century property developers found it more profitable to remodel the premises.

The Intimate, the Grand ...

The Palais de Justice, today a complex of buildings encompassing the centralized legal machinery of modern France, is still redolent of the past. The nation's earliest kings (who dwelt here) and later the nobility and Revolutionary leaders who were imprisoned here before execution, still seem to haunt the corridors. The Palais also conceals a Gothic masterpiece, the **Sainte-Chapelle**, whose beautiful stained glass

Bridging Paris

The 27 bridges spanning the Seine form a wonderful collection, but four are especially worthy of your attention.

The **Pont-Neuf** (or 'new' bridge) is in fact the oldest bridge in Paris, completed by Henri IV in 1606. It was the first one built without houses: Parisians were pleased to walk across and see their river. It soon became a favourite spot for promenades and a whole plethora of street-singers, charlatans, amateur dentists, professional ladies, pickpockets and, above all, for the *bouquinistes* selling their old books and pamphlets out of boxes. Established booksellers on the Ile de la Cité were enraged and drove them off to the banks of the Seine, where they have remained ever since.

The **Pont-Royal**, built for Louis XIV in 1685, commands a splendid panorama of the Tuileries Gardens and the Louvre. It is the capital's most central bridge in the sense that it offers good views of the Grand and Petit Palais, two '*grands bourgeois*' buildings, and the Ecole des Beaux-Arts and Institut de France, favoured by the intellectual community.

The **Pont de la Concorde**, *the* bridge of the French Revolution, went up between 1787 and 1790. Its framework used stones from the dismantled Bastille prison – particularly galling for the Royalists in that it was originally called Pont Louis XVI. The name was duly changed to Pont de la Révolution the year before Louis was guillotined, a few steps from the bridge, on the Place de la Concorde.

The **Pont Alexandre III**'s single steel arch is its main architectural distinction. The bridge represents the final flowering of that proud 19th-century industrial spirit, best exemplified by the Eiffel Tower. The Tsar of Russia, Nicholas II, laid the first stone in 1896; the bridge was completed at the turn of the century. Purists find its statues to Fame and Pegasus insufferably bombastic, but lovers view them as an appropriately melodramatic touch to a moonlit stroll beneath the bridge's Belle-Epoque lanterns. Try not to disturb sleeping *clochards*.

and harmonious proportions stand in sharp contrast to the ponderous palace. The chapel was built in 1248 by the pious King Louis IX (known as St Louis) to house the Crown of Thorns and a fragment of the True Cross, obtained from the Emperor of Constantinople. The 15 **stained-glass windows** include 1,134 different pieces, depicting mainly Old Testament scenes; 720 of them are 13th-century originals. The setting could hardly be bettered for concerts.

Between 1789 and 1815 the chapel assumed the various guises of a flour warehouse during the Revolution and a club-house for high-ranking dandies, before serving as an archive for Napoleon's Consulate. It was this latter role that saved the chapel from projected destruction, because the bureaucrats did not know where else to put their mountains of paperwork.

These days, they find room in the Palais de Justice and the nearby Préfecture de Police. What started off in 360 as the site of Julian's coronation as the Emperor of Rome, later housing Merovingian kings Clovis, Childebert, Chilpéric and Dagobert, is now strictly Maigret country. The great Salle des Pas Perdus is worth a visit for a glimpse of the lawyers, plaintiffs, witnesses, court reporters and hangers-on waiting nervously for the wheels of French justice to grind into action.

... and the Gruesome

But their anxiety is nothing compared with those who were condemned to bide their time in the **Conciergerie**, reached from the Quai de l'Horloge. After 6 April 1793, at the height of the Revolutionary Terror, the Conciergerie (named after the royally appointed concierge in charge of common-law criminals) truly became the 'antechamber

The Conciergerie, on the Quai de l'Horloge, remains inextricably linked with the days of the Revolutionary Terror.

30

of the guillotine'. In the Galerie des Prisonniers, Marie-Antoinette, Robespierre (who had sent many others there), Saint-Just and Danton all spent their last nights, after the Revolutionary tribunals had passed sentence.

The Salle des Girondins displays one of the guillotine blades, the crucifux to which Marie-Antoinette prayed before execution and the lock from Robespierre's cell. Look out on the Cour des Femmes and see where husbands, lovers, wives and mistresses were allowed one last tryst before the tumbrels came. About 2,500 victims of the Revolutionary guillotine spent their final hours in the Conciergerie.

Notre-Dame de Paris

The site of the **Cathedral of Notre-Dame de Paris** has had a religious significance for at least 2,000 years. In Roman times a temple to Jupiter stood here; some stone fragments of the early structure, unearthed in 1711, can be seen in the Musée de Cluny (see p.58). In

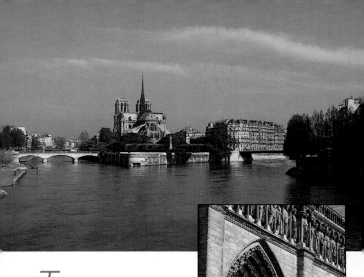

The Cathedral of Notre-Dame stands proudly on the Ile de la Cité, at the very heart of Paris. Right: the cathedral's doorways.

the 4th century the first Christian church, Saint-Etienne, was built here, joined two centuries later by a second church, dedicated to Notre Dame. Norman invasions of Paris left the two edifices in a sorry state, and the Bishop Maurice de Sully authorized the construction of a cathedral to replace them in 1163. The main part of Notre-Dame took 167 years to complete, and the transition it represented from Romanesque to Gothic has been called a perfect expression of medieval architecture. One dissenting voice was that of St Bernard, who protested that the godly virtue of poverty would be insulted by the erection of such a sumptuous structure.

Old Baron Haussmann comes in again for a dose of criticism because he greatly enlarged the *parvis*, or square, in front of the cathedral, thereby diminishing the grandiose impact of the western façade. Others argue that this brought back the animated street life of the square, recapturing some of the spirit of the Middle Ages, when the *parvis* was used for public executions and the populace was invited to throw old fruit and rotten eggs kindly provided by the authorities.

The cathedral remains an impressive monument, truly the nation's parish church. It has been the setting for some momentous events in French history: in 1239 Louis IX walked barefoot through the cathedral with his holy treasure, Christ's Crown of Thorns (before the Sainte-Chapelle was built); in 1430 it saw the humiliating crowning ceremony of Henry VI of England as King of France; in 1594 Henri IV attended the mass that sealed his conversion to Catholicism and reinforced his hold on the French throne; and it is here also that in 1804 Napoleon's coronation as Emperor took place (the Pope attended the ceremony but was upstaged by Napoleon crowning himself). More recently, the cathedral held the state funerals of military heroes such as Foch, Leclerc and de Gaulle.

Given the cathedral's gigantic size, the balance of its proportions and the harmony of its façade are nothing short of miraculous. The superb central **rose window** encircling the statue of the *Madonna and Child* depicts the Redemption after the Fall. Look for the **Galerie des Rois** across the top of the three doorways. The 28 statues representing the kings of Judah and Israel were pulled down during the Revolution because they were thought to be of **33** the kings of France (they were later restored).

Inside, the marvellous lighting is due in large part to two more outsize rose windows, dominating the transept. Don't miss the lovely 14th-century **Virgin and Child** that bears the cathedral's name, Notre-Dame de Paris, to the right of the choir entrance.

The original architect remains anonymous, but the renowned Pierre de Montreuil (also active on the Sainte-Chapelle work site) was responsible for much of the 13th-century work. The present structure, with its majestic towers, spire and breathtaking flying-buttresses, owes much to the hard labour of Eugène Viollet-le-Duc, who worked patiently over the whole edifice between 1845 and 1863, restoring the cathedral after the ravages of the 18th century. This time, pre-Revolutionary meddlers bent on redecorating and 'improving' are to blame, rather than the Revolutionaries.

All the original bells have disappeared with the exception of the *bourdon*, dating from 1400, in the south tower. Its much-admired purity of tone was achieved in the 1680s when the bronze bell was melted down and mixed with the gold and silver jewellery donated by Louis XIV's aristocracy. Today it is no longer operated by a hunchback but by an electric system installed in 1953.

The climb up the tower may be quite strenuous, but because of its perfect central position, the cathedral affords magnificent views of Paris, stretching inland from the Seine as it threads its way through the city.

ILE SAINT-LOUIS

Though linked by a bridge, the sister islands could not be further apart in spirit. The Ile Saint-Louis is an enchanted, self-contained island of gracious living, long popular with Paris's affluent gentry. President Georges Pompidou lived here (on the Quai de Béthune) and loved to come here from the Elysée Palace as often as he possibly could.

Appropriate to the island's stylish reputation, its church, the **Saint-Louis-en-l'Ile** is as elegant as one of its great mansions. It is bright and airy, and a golden light illuminates a marvellous collection of Dutch, Flemish and Italian 16th- and 17th-century art as well as some splendid tapestries from the 12th century.

The most striking of the mansions, the **Hôtel Lauzun**, at 17 Quai d'Anjou, was built in the 1650s by the great architect Louis le Vau, who also worked on the Seine façade of the Louvre and on the Versailles château. The **Hôtel Lambert**, another impressive 17th-century mansion designed by Le Vau for the Sun-King's secretary, stands on the corner of the Rue Saint-Louis-en-l'Ile. Voltaire once enjoyed a tempestuous love affair here with the lady of the house, the marquise du Châtelet.

But perhaps the island's greatest pleasure consists of walking along the poplar-shaded streets to the western end of the Quai d'Orléans. There you will have the most stunning **view** of the apse of Notre-Dame, which incorrigible romantics much prefer to the cathedral's 'front'. The queues will indicate the way to Berthillon, Paris's foremost ice-cream maker, with its 60 flavours. Worth queueing for.

Fans of Berthillon's delicious ice creams flock to the Ile Saint-Louis.

Right Bank

POMP AND CIRCUMSTANCE

(L'Etoile–Concorde–Palais-Royal)

The Right Bank runs the gamut of very chic to slightly murky, taking in Montmartre on the way. It covers a good deal of the most renowned and fashionable shopping areas, the *grands boulevards*, seamy Clichy and Pigalle, the embassies and the Elysée Palace, the financial district around the Bourse, but also La Défense with its new Grande Arche, the Louvre, the Tuileries, the Marais, the Jewish quarter, the up-and-coming Bastille, and much more.

Star Sights

Any tour of the Right Bank should begin at the **Place de l'Etoile** (officially Place Charles-de-Gaulle), preferably on top of the **Arc de Triomphe**. One reason for climbing up Napoleon's gigantic tri-

umphal arch (50m high and 45m wide, or 164ft by 148ft) is to get a good view of the 12-pointed star (*étoile*), formed by 12 avenues radiating from the arch in a *tour de force* of geometric planning. A satellite ring of important streets neatly surrounds the Etoile like a spider's web. The *place*, a vast sloping mound at the top of a gentle rise, cannot really be taken in at ground level, nor its stunning beauty appreciated. The monumental ensemble, conceived by Napoleon as a tribute to France's military glories and heroes, was completed by Haussmann. Over the years, the arch has taken on a mythic quality, as successive regimes have invested it with the spirit of the nation, whether republican or imperial.

Napoleon himself saw only a life-size model made of wood and canvas. The Etoile's monumental ensemble was completed for Napoleon III by Baron Haussmann. It became the traditional focus for state funerals of national political, military and literary heroes – Victor Hugo was given a positively pharaonic tribute here after his death in 1885. In 1920, the Unknown Soldier of World War I was buried at the arch, and three years later the eternal flame was lit. When Hitler came to Paris as a conqueror in 1940, this was the first place he wanted to see. Naturally, at the Liberation, this was where

Street Name-Dropping

What's in a name? In Paris, street names often change according to political sensitivities and popular feelings – a clear sign of their importance. In the 12th century under Philippe Auguste, Paris counted 300 muddy twisting streets. Today, 5,250 boulevards, avenues, squares, streets, passages, galleries and cul-de-sacs (impasses) narrate the history of the capital and, by extension, France.

The names themselves only 'stuck' from the 17th century onward. It was then a new way for municipalities to honour their illustrious forebears – or more often to kowtow to the high and mighty of the day. Before that, streets were known by the colourful names given them by the populace.

If the army gets a good slice of the cake (50-odd generals), the church comes out with three times as many. There is even an Impasse Satan (so tiny most maps don't mention it) and a Passage d'Enfer (Hell's Way) – appropriately one-way only. Luckily, there's also an Impasse Dieu – not to be confused with the Rue Dieu, named after a Napoleonic general.

For a somewhat hypochondriac nation, the fact that 40-odd streets are named after doctors is not surprising, but women are not given the gallant treatment one would expect (Jeanne d'Arc and George Sand, however, make it). The French, inveterate wine-lovers, naturally baptise some of their streets with favourite appellations controlées, like Graves, while ladies of easy virtue gave the name of their profession to plenty of sordid streets. These have been toned down since, but Parisians, who never respect anything, go on calling them by their old name anyway.

General de Gaulle started his triumphant march down the Champs-Elysées.

Avenue Foch, leading away from the Etoile to the Bois de Boulogne, is one of the most majestic of the city's residential avenues and the best of Baron Haussmann's conceptions. One of the most exclusive, too, though somewhat democratized these days by the *boules* players on its gravelled side paths. Avenue de la Grande-Armée points straight to Neuilly and at the end, the towers of La Défense with the Grande Arche behind, forming part of a complete east-west axis for Paris, now nearing completion.

It's fashionable nowadays to look down on the **Champs-Elysées** (Parisians yarn about how long they *haven't* set foot there), but despite extensive commercialization it remains one of the finest avenues any-

The Obelisk on the Place de la Concorde is the oldest monument in Paris.

where in the world: straight as a rod, stretching at a fairly gentle incline all the way down to the Place de la Concorde and fringed by chestnut trees, the avenue is the object of careful planning. More trees are currently being planted along the Champs-Elysées to ensure that it retains its elegant beauty.

The first two-thirds of the avenue are devoted to cinemas, gleaming airline offices and car showrooms, shopping galleries, shops and café terraces. The best vantage points for people-watching lie between the Avenue George-V and the Rue Lincoln on the 'shady' side, and in the Rue Colisée on the 'sunny' side.

After the Rond-Point, the mood changes and a pleasant manicured park leads you down towards the Place de la Concorde past two major landmarks: the **Petit Palais**, all steel and glass, and the **Grand Palais**. Both were built for the World Fair of 1900 and are now devoted to large-scale exhibitions of great masters, though the Petit Palais does have some private permanent collections of 19th-century French masters. The Grand Palais shares its colossal building with the museum of the Palais de la Découverte, given over to the sciences. Astronomy takes pride of place in the museum, with the planetarium as its centre-piece; there, you can watch 9,000 stars and planets roam around the ceiling.

Even today, the **Place de la Concorde** scarcely deserves its name – more motorists come to grief here than anywhere else in Paris. Barely surprising – it takes solid nerves to hurl one's vehicle into the vast arena. Its past record is hardly less impressive: more than 1,000 people were guillotined here during the Revolution; in 1934 it was the scene of bloody rioting against the government; and ten years later it was the Nazis' last hold in Paris.

The spacious *place*, of unmatched grace and elegance, was designed by Jacques-Ange Gabriel in 1753, but the Revolution soon disposed of all royal connotations. Gone was its original name (Place Louis XV), as was the king's **39** statue, replaced by the guillotine. Statues representing eight of France's regional capitals top the eight plinths, while the two imposing statues that guard the opening on to the Champ-Elysées are the famous *Chevaux de Marly*, sculpted by Coustou between 1740 and 1745. (They will shortly go into the new wing of the Louvre.) Plumb in the centre, you'll see Paris's oldest monument, the 23m (75ft) high pink syenite-granite Obelisk of Luxor from the temple of Ramses II, dating back to 1300 BC and erected here in 1836. For a change, it's not something that Napoleon brought back from his campaigns, but a gift from Mohammed Ali, viceroy of Egypt.

Pleasure Gardens

After the bustle of the Avenue des Champs-Elysées and the Place de la Concorde, take refuge in the cool shade of the chestnut trees in the **Jardin des Tuileries**, named after 13th-century tileworks. The impressive size of the garden is due in large part to the destruction of the Palais des Tuileries during the 1871 Commune (fragments can still be seen by the Jeu de Paume in the north-west corner). Children will enjoy donkey rides, puppet shows in spring and summer and sailing their boats in the circular pond. On the river side of the Tuileries, the **Orangerie** is best known for its ground-floor rooms, decorated with Monet's beautiful *Nymphéas* murals, but take a look too at the excellent collection of works by Cézanne, Renoir, Utrillo, Le Douanier Rousseau and Picasso, housed upstairs in the Jean Walther-Paul Guillaume Collection.

At the eastern end of the Tuileries stands the pink **Arc de Triomphe du Carrousel**, built at roughly the same time as its bigger brother at the Etoile, and visible in a straight line beyond the Obelisk. This imposing effect was originally planned for Napoleon to admire from his bedroom in the Louvre. Today, the vista is somewhat spoiled by the hazy phalanx of modern sky-

Leafy Retreat

The chic 16th arrondissement has its very own playground in the shape of the Bois de Boulogne. More blithely known by residents of the western parts of the city as *Le Bois*, the 9,000sq km (3,475sq miles) site is what remains of the old Rouvray forest. It was left to go wild until 1852, when Napoleon turned it into a place of recreation for the people of Paris.

Baron Haussmann's transformations of the Bois rank among his happier achievements, and it is now the closest thing Paris has to a London-style park. One of the main attractions is the Parc de Bagatelle, a walled English garden with the city's most magnificent display of flowers.

Children enjoy the Jardin d'Acclimatation with its miniature train, Punch and Judy show, pony rides and miniature farm. With lakes, greenery and horse-racing just next door, you could be miles away from the city.

But at sundown the Bois de Boulogne puts on a different face, as transvestites turn the place into a very dubious area indeed. AIDS concern has resulted in a severe clampdown on nocturnal activities. The Bois now shuts down after 8 p.m., at which time it becomes strictly out of bounds.

scrapers of La Défense looming on the horizon. Extensive works on the underground parking and shopping complex and the restoration of the Richelieu wing of the Louvre somewhat isolate the Carrousel, but in a few years' time the promenade from the Place de la Concorde through the Tuileries, past the Louvre all the way to the church of Saint-Germain l'Auxerrois, will be perfectly stunning.

Go by the Louvre Museum, taking in its sweeping majesty (for a separate visit, see p.83), and cross the Rue de Rivoli to the **Palais-Royal**. Built as Cardinal Richelieu's residence in 1639, it was originally named the Palais Cardinal (it became

41

'royal' when Anne d'Autriche moved in with young Louis XIV). This serene, timeless, arcaded palace, with its garden of lime trees and beeches – and the pond where Louis XIV nearly drowned – has always been a colourful centre of more or less respectable activity. It housed the first 'Italian' theatre in Paris, where Corneille's *Le Cid* was performed.

In the days of Philippe d'Orléans, Regent of France during Louis XV's minority, the Palais-Royal was the scene of notorious orgies. To meet the Orleans' extravagant debts, some ground-floor rooms were turned into boutiques and cafés that attracted a fashionable society. (Today, these shops still exist, selling coins, medals, tin soldiers and antiques.) Some shady hangers-on also became regular visitors: artists, charlatans, prostitutes, pickpockets – and intellectuals. On 13 July 1789 a young firebrand orator, Camille Desmoulins, stood on a table at the Palais-Royal's Café de Foy to make the call to arms that set off the French Revolution. After Waterloo, Prussian General Blücher arrived to blow 1,500,000 francs in one night at one of the many rambunctuous gambling dens.

The Palais-Royal then fell out of fashion, as the crowds headed north to the *grands boulevards*, and eventually became a very respectable place favoured by artists and writers. Colette lived there.

The Ministry of Culture now looks down on the **Buren columns**. These controversial black and white marble columns, truncated at varying heights, were erected in the main courtyard in 1986. While some are just the right height for seats and others lend themselves to the games of children, only dogs seem to love them all indifferently.

Halls of Fame

Two venerable institutions worthy of note stand behind the Palais-Royal: the **Banque de France** and the **Bibliothèque Nationale** (National Library) – the brand new TGB

Give free rein to your imagination and see what you can make of the Buren columns.

(*Très Grande Bibliothèque* or Very Large Library), currently underway on the Left Bank, will soon bring welcome support to its older counterpart. The idea of a royal library was born in 1368, when Charles V installed 973 manuscripts in his library in the Louvre, but it was François I who acquired new material and had Oriental, Latin and Greek manuscripts copied, and who made it all available to scholars. He also issued a law in 1573 whereby the right to print any work required donating a copy to the king's library. The library moved to its present premises in 1570 but it has had to grow non-stop to house the 10 million books and periodicals, 12 million engravings, 650,000 maps and over 350,000 ancient manuscripts, one of which is Charlemagne's *Evangéliaire*.

East again of the Palais-Royal, the old food markets of Les Halles (transferred to the more hygienic, if less colourful, suburb of Rungis) have been replaced by delightful gardens, new apartment blocks **43** and the **Forum des Halles**, a popular, tubular shopping centre.

Around it, lively neighbourhood cafés, boutiques and art galleries link up with the Centre Pompidou. The liveliest meeting place is around the handsome Renaissance **Fontaine des Innocents** (once part of a cemetery). The nearby Rue Saint-Denis is slightly seedy, and notorious for the ladies of easy virtue who ply their trade.

On the north side of Les Halles another massive monument of the Renaissance period, but decidedly Gothic in silhouette, is the church of **Saint-Eustache**, remarkable for its 17th-century stained-glass windows, crafted according to medieval traditions.

WEALTH AND OPULENCE

(Place Vendome–Opéra–Madeleine)
Still on the Right Bank, but inland this time, Paris displays more architectural treasures and leafy retreats.

Opulence positively exudes from the **Place Vendôme**. Louis XIV wanted the perfect setting for a square that would set off a statue of his own royal self. He found it in the then Hôtel Vendôme, and on 16 August 1699 a statue of the king on horse-back was erected in the middle of the airy, gracious octagonal square. As for the houses around the Place Vendôme, only Louis' financiers could afford the rents. Today, the Ministry of Justice shares the *place* with a handful of international banks, some of

Fountains of Charity

Not only did English philanthropist Sir Richard Wallace endow London with a fabulous gallery, but he also bestowed his bounties on the French capital. Born in 1818, he spent some of his youth in Paris, and donated 66 fountains to the city at a time when public hygiene was a subject of great concern. He designed them himself: the four caryatides symbolize Simplicity, Beauty, Sobriety and Charity. They stand on a base of bronze, engraved with dolphins that reappear at the top of the dome. Weighing in at 700kg (some 1,400lb) and nearly 2.7m (8ft) tall, the fountains gush 4,000 litres (7,000 pints) of water a day. Over the years, some have disappeared or been destroyed, but they are still a prominent feature in Paris. You will see them along the main popular arteries, as on the Boulevard Richard-Lenoir, for instance, and water still pours forth from them, as it did when they were first installed. The only change is that the goblets and chains were removed in 1952 – again, out of concern for public health. The same firm that made the first fountain in 1873, the Sommevoire foundry, continues to make them.

the greatest Parisian jewellers and the Ritz.

Like all royal statues, that of Louis XIV was overthrown during the Revolution. A later addition, the spiral of bronze bas-reliefs on the Vendôme column, commemorating Napoleon's victories and topped by a statue of the Emperor himself, was cast from 1,250 cannons captured from the Austrians at Austerlitz.

Window-shop your way past the goldsmiths and furriers of the Rue de la Paix to the **Opéra-Garnier** – a massive monument by Charles Garnier, characteristic of the pomp and ceremony of Napoleon III's Second Empire. Construction work started at the height of **45**

The Opéra-Garnier (above), and a detail of the ceiling, by Lenepveu (right).

Napoleon's reign in 1862, when Paris boasted of being Europe's most glamorous capital, but the Opéra was not completed until 1875, after the Commune. 'It has no style; it's neither Greek nor Roman,' complained the Empress Eugénie. 'It's Napoléon III style,' retorted the architect. Garnier used all the latest building techniques, including ironwork. (The same techniques were used for Les Halles and the Eiffel Tower, in the same period.) Its neo-Baroque style is less of an aesthetic joy than a bombastic statement, proclaiming the triumph of the French bourgeoisie. The public rooms and the staircase were conceived in a grand manner – more so even than the auditorium, which holds only 2,000 spectators. Today, spectators crane their necks to study the vast colourful ceiling painted by Chagall in 1964.

Like the Opéra, the **grands boulevards** have gone somewhat out of fashion since the turn of the century, but their bustle and sweep are still evocative of their former glory. On the Boulevard des Capucines, you can retrace the footsteps of Renoir, Manet and Pissarro taking their paintings to Nadar's house, at no. 35, for the historic 1874 exhibition of Impressionism. Today, the boulevards house some of the town's most popular cinemas – appropriately enough, for it is here, at the Hôtel Scribe, that the Lumière brothers staged the first public moving-theatre show in 1895.

Variously conceived as a stock exchange, the Bank of France and a theatre, the **Madeleine** may not look like a church but that's what it is. Napoleon's first instinct was to turn it into a Temple de la Gloire for his Great Army, but his architect persuaded him to build the Arc de Triomphe instead. The restored monarchy opted for a church, as originally planned under Louis XV. The huge Greco-Roman edifice, consecrated only in 1842, was left without a transept, bell-tower, aisles or even a cross on the roof. Parisians like it most for the grand **view** from the steps down the Rue Royale to the Place de la Concorde. Step inside, however, and the deeply religious atmosphere in a *quartier* totally given over to materialism is nothing less than startling.

MONTMARTRE

Topographically, Montmartre is still the little country village of 400 years ago, full of narrow, winding streets and dead-ends. Don't take a car there; use the Montmartrobus to discover it in a single tour, or take the metro to Abbesses – don't get off at Pigalle; however **47**

attractive its lurid glitter at night, by day it might put you off getting to Montmartre at all.

Head up the Rue Ravignan to no. 13 Place Emile Goudeau, site of the unprepossessing studio of the **Bateau-Lavoir**. It is here, if anywhere, that modern art was born: Picasso, Braque and Juan Gris developed Cubism, Modigliani, meanwhile, painted in a style all of his own, and Apollinaire wrote his first surrealistic verses. Nearby, the illustrious predecessors of these upstarts – Renoir, Van Gogh and Gauguin – lived and worked in the Rue Cortot, Rue de l'Abreuvoir, Rue Saint-Rustique (site of the restaurant *A la Bonne Franquette* where Van Gogh painted his famous *La Guinguette*). As for Utrillo and his mother, Suzanne Valadon, they were '*montmartrois*' born and bred.

In artistic terms, you go from the sublime to the ridiculous at the old Place du Tertre. This is the very centre of Montmartre's village life, where marriages were announced, militia men enlisted and criminals hanged. Try and visit it in the early morning – before the 'artists' set up their easels and the crowds take over.

On the Rue Saint-Vincent at the corner of the Rue des Saules, look out for Paris's own vineyard, the Clos de Montmartre, whose wine reputedly makes you 'jump like a goat'.

At the other end of the Rue Saint-Vincent you come round the back of the Sacré-Cœur basilica. This weird Romano-Byzantine church has a dubious reputation. Aesthetes scorn its over-ornate exterior and extravagant mosaics; working-class people of the *quartier* resent the way it was put up as a symbol of penitence for the insurrection of the 1871 Commune and defeat in the war against the Prussians. The miraculously white façade derives from its special Château-Landon stone that whitens to the contact with carbonic gas and hardens with age. For many, the church's only redeeming feature is the view of the city from the dome or the terrace below.

Cimetière du Père Lachaise

Such is the capital's pride in the great of its past that cemeteries enjoy a special place in Paris. The Père-Lachaise, the most famous of Parisian resting places, has a population estimated at 1,350,000 buried here since its foundation in 1804. The neat avenues of tombs provide a fascinating walk through history, though you may prefer to take a guided tour in a little vehicle.

Named after Louis XIV's confessor, a member of the Jesuits who previously owned the land, the cemetery has long been renowned as the resting place for the heroes of the country's revolutions. It even served as a battleground on 28 May 1871 for the last stand of the Communards, and a 'Mur des Fédérés' at the south-east corner marks the place where they were executed by firing squads. Napoleon's emancipation of the Jews meant that they could have their own section, and Napoleon III's deference to the Turkish ambassador for his Eastern foreign policy led to an area for Muslims. Presidents of the Third Republic, like Adolphe Thiers, lie just a stone's throw away from the Radicals they bitterly opposed – the Père-Lachaise is a great leveller.

A little map available at the entrance will help you locate the most famous tombs, including recent 'arrivals' such as Yves Montand, now resting beside Simone Signoret, and, shrine among shrines, Jim Morrison's. He's in fine company. In this pantheon of the city's artistic heritage, you will find writers Colette and Alfred de Musset and Italian composer Rossini at *lot* no. 4, Chopin (11), philosopher Auguste Comte (17), painters Ingres (23), Corot and Daumier (24), La Fontaine and Molière (25), Sarah Bernhardt (44), Balzac (48) Delacroix (49), Bizet (68) Proust (85), Apollinaire (86), Isadora Duncan (87), and Oscar Wilde (89), whose tomb is a fine monument by sculptor Jacob Epstein.

Just down the hill from the Sacré-Cœur is **Saint-Pierre-de-Montmartre**, which is one of Paris's oldest churches. Consecrated in 1147, 16 years before the church of Saint-Germain-des-Prés (see p.61), it represents a significant work of early Gothic art, belied by its 18th-century façade. The Sacré-Cœur's architect, Paul Abadie, wanted to demolish Saint-Pierre, but he was overruled, and it was restored 'as a riposte to the Sacré-Cœur'.

THE MARAIS

The Marais district, north of the Ile de la Cité and Ile Saint-Louis, has bravely withstood the onslaught of modern construction. It provides a remarkably authentic record of the development of Paris, from the reign of Henri IV at the end of the 16th century to the advent of the Revolution. Built on reclaimed marshland as its names suggests, it contains some of Europe's most elegant

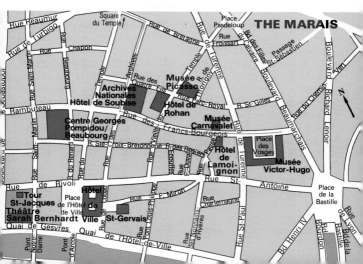

Renaissance houses (*hôtels*), which now serve as museums and libraries. The Marais has recently become fashionable again and trendy boutiques spring up seemingly every day.

Take the metro to Rambuteau and start at the corner of the Rue des Archives and Rue des Francs-Bourgeois, named after the poor people allowed to live here tax-free in the 14th century. The national archives are kept here in an 18th-century mansion, the **Hôtel de Soubise**. Across a vast, horseshoe-shaped courtyard, you come across the exquisite Roccoco style of Louis XV's times, in the apartments of the Prince and Princess of Soubise. Up on the first floor is the **Musée de l'Histoire de France**. There you will find such gems as the only known portrait of Jeanne d'Arc painted in her lifetime and the diary of Louis XVI, where you can read his entry for 14 July 1789, the day the Bastille was stormed: '*Rien*' (nothing).

A garden (not always open to the public) connects the Hôtel de Soubise with its twin brother, the **Hôtel de Rohan**, on the Rue Vieille du Temple. Both were designed by Pierre-Alexis Delamair. Look out for Pierre Le Lorrain's fine sculpture of *Les Chevaux d'Apollon*, over the old stables in the second courtyard. The piece is widely considered to be the most beautiful 18th-century sculpture in France.

Two other mansions worthy of your attention on the Rue des Francs-Bourgeois are the **Hôtel Lamoignon**, at the corner of the Rue Pavée, and the **Hôtel Carnavalet**, home of the illustrious lady of letters, Madame de Sévigné and now the **Musée Historique de la Ville de Paris** (closed on Mondays). The documents, engravings and paintings displayed bring Paris's history to life. The outstanding exhibit devoted to the Revolution includes a letter from Robespierre dramatically stained

52

The Place des Vosges is a model of architectural grace.

with the author's blood: he was arrested and wounded while signing it.

The **Musée Picasso**, round the corner at 5 Rue Thorigny, is housed in the beautifully restored Hôtel Salé. The museum received over 200 paintings and 158 sculptures, in addition to hundreds of drawings, engravings, ceramics and models for stage sets and costumes, from the private collections of Picasso's heirs. The museum also exhibits the artist's own collection of master works by fellow painters Braque, Matisse, Miró, Degas, Renoir and Rousseau. But most moving are the private relics on display: letters, photo albums, bullfight tickets and holiday postcards amongst others.

With a fine dramatic sense, the Rue des Francs-Bourgeois ends at what many consider to be the city's most handsome residential square, the **Place des Vosges**. Henri IV had it built in 1605 on the site of a

horse-market. Henri's 'idea' (he copied it from Catherine de Médici) was to have a vast square with 'all the houses built in the same symmetry'. The gardens – once a favourite spot for the aristocratic duel and, after Louis XIII's wedding festivities in this spot, the town's most fashionable promenade – are now a pleasant children's playground. Louis XIII's statue was melted down during the Revolution but replaced in 1818.

The best time to see the square is in the winter, when the lovely chestnut trees are bare and don't obscure the pretty pink façades. In pre-Revolutionary days the square used to be known as the Place Royale; it received its current name for the simple reason that the *département* of the Vosges was the first to pay up all its taxes to the Revolutionary government. Victor Hugo, the great writer, used to live at no. 6 and his house has been turned into a fascinating museum housing his manuscripts, artefacts, desk and **54** some wonderful drawings.

*D*ay and night, Saint-Michel buzzes with life.

New Trends

Finish your visit to the Marais with a walk round the old **Jewish quarter** (or *shtetl*, as the Paris Jews call it). Jews have lived around the Rue des Rosiers continuously from 1230, and the Rue Ferdinand Duval was known until 1900 as the Rue des Juifs. The other main street of the *shtetl*, Rue des Ecouffes (a medieval slang word for moneylender), completes the lively shopping area. Jews from North Africa are gradually replacing the Ashkenzani of Eastern Europe, who themselves took over from the Sephardim. Delicatessens and *falafel* shops keep the district nicely 'ecumenical'.

The spacious, circular **Place de la Bastille** is enjoying a new lease of life. Nothing remains of the infamous prison and the column in the centre

commemorates the Revolution of 1830. As it is today, it's mostly mid-19th century, with trendy art galleries and artists' studios springing up in the adjacent streets. Long a rather run-down area, the spacious Place has obtained its **Opéra-Bastille**, the new opera house, which has brought it back in focus. The much criticized exterior hides a stark decor and some wonderful acoustics. Take a guided **tour** and try to go to a show. Afterwards, you can wander round the Rue de la Lappe and other nearby streets, teeming with life.

Left Bank

Contrary to common belief, not all the Left Bank is given over to the *Quartier Latin* or student precincts, though most of the capital's young brain-power is concentrated here. A tour of the Left Bank should start with the Latin Quarter, however, if only to get an idea of what the *rive gauche* is about – you will find every-thing concentrated there, from the down-and-out to the ultra-chic. As for intellectual snob-bery, it is fact far more prevalent *left* of the Left Bank than in the Latin Quarter itself. **55**

LATIN QUARTER

Just over the bridge from Notre-Dame is where it all begins. Here, the spirit of inquiry has traditionally been nurtured, sometimes leading to protest and outright revolt before subsiding into lifelong scepticism, as the rebels graduate from the university and move west to the more genteel Faubourg Saint-Germain. As far back as the 13th century, when the city's first 'university' moved from the cloisters of Notre-Dame to the Left Bank, the young came to the *quartier* – originally to learn Latin.

In those days the university simply meant a collection of people – students who met on a street corner, in a public square or a courtyard to hear a lecture given from a bench or balcony. Today there are overcrowded

Café Culture

Whereas some *quartiers* are known for their palaces and churches, Montparnasse (named after a 17th-century gravel mound, since removed) has cafés and bars for landmarks. The Closerie des Lilas, a watering hole for French Symbolist poets at the turn of the century, served as a meeting place for Trotsky and Lenin before World War I and for Hemingway and his friends after the war; the Select, the first all-night bar to open in Montparnasse in 1925, quickly became a Henry Miller hangout; La Coupole, favoured by Sartre and Simone de Beauvoir, is still going strong after its radical revamp in the late 1980s (it's more a living theatre than a restaurant); breakfast was taken at the Dôme for a change of scenery; the Rotonde, favoured by Picasso, André Derain, Maurice Vlaminck, Modigliani and Max Jacob, is still a popular restaurant, next to a cinema of the same name. In one way or another, most of them have managed to survive along the bustling, ever-changing Boulevard Montparnasse.

classrooms, but the tradition of open-air discussion continues, often over a coffee or a mineral water on a café terrace in the Boulevard Saint-Michel, the streets around the faculty buildings, or in the ever-present cinema queues.

Begin at the **Place Saint-Michel**, where Parisian students still come to buy their textbooks and stationery, and foreign students come to sniff the Latin Quarter's mystique, gathering round the bombastic 1860s fountain by Davioud. Plunge into the narrow streets of the **Saint-Séverin** quarter – to the east, Rues Saint-Séverin, de la Harpe and Galande. You will discover a medieval world updated by the varied exotica of Tunisian pastry shops, smoky Greek barbecues and stuffy little cinemas. In this Levantine atmosphere **Saint-Julien-le-Pauvre**, one of Paris's most modest churches but also one of its oldest, hardly stands out as odd with its incense wafting and its Sunday mass said in Greek or Arabic (this is not a Roman Catholic church but a Melchite

one). A moment's meditation in the exquisite 13th–15th-century Flamboyant Gothic **church of Saint-Séverin**, where Dante is said to have prayed and Saint-Saëns asked to be honorary organist, and you are ready to confront the Latin Quarter's citadel, the **Sorbonne.**

Founded in 1253 as a college for poor theological students by Robert de Sorbon, Louis IX's chaplain, the university was later taken in hand by Cardinal Richelieu, who financed its reconstruction (1624–42). You can visit the grand amphitheatre (2,700 seats), with its statues of Sorbon, Richelieu, Descartes, Pascal and Lavoisier, the great chemist. As you look at Puvis de Chavannes' monumental painting covering the back wall, *Le Bois Sacré* – an allegorical interpretation of Poetry, History, Geology, Physiology and the rest – try to imagine the scene of May 1968. The student revolt against overcrowding, antiquated teaching, bureaucracy and the very basis of the social system **57** made the Sorbonne the focal point of the movement. When the police invaded the sanctuary – which for centuries had guaranteed student immunity – the rebellion was on.

Almost facing the Sorbonne's Rue des Ecoles entrance is the **Musée de Cluny** (6 Place Paul-Painlevé). It's the best place to see the city's beginnings. Within its grounds are the remains of the Roman public baths, the Thermes de Cluny, dating from AD 200–300. Older still are the fragments of a monument to Jupiter (probably from the 1st century AD) found near the Cathedral of Notre-Dame. The fine Flamboyant chapel harbours a remarkable Saint-Etienne tapestry, but the most celebrated tapestry in the museum is the 16th-century **Boussac series**, the *Lady with the Unicorn.*

A stroll up the Rue Saint-Jacques past the most famous high school in Paris, the Lycée Louis le Grand, leads to the gigantic neo-Classic **Panthéon**. The resting place of the nation's literary, military and political figures, it stands as a

dignified reminder to students of what hard work can achieve. Originally designed as the church of Sainte-Geneviève for Louis XV (1755), it was secularized during the Revolution as a vast mausoleum with the inscription: 'To our great men, the Motherland's gratitude'. But the Revolutionaries had a hard time deciding who deserved the honour. (Mirabeau and Marat rested there for a while, before being expelled.) Napoleon ended the

controversy by turning it back into a church. Throughout the 19th century it went back and forth between secular and consecrated status, according to the régime's political colour. Finally Victor Hugo's funeral in 1885 settled the Panthéon's status as a secular mausoleum once and for all. He was followed (retroactively) by Voltaire and Rousseau, and then by prime minister Léon Gambetta, socialist leader Jean Jaurès, Emile Zola, Louis Braille (inventor of the blind alphabet), President Raymond Poincaré and many others.

Taking a Break

After all this might and majesty, take a break in the **Jardins du Luxembourg**. If you want to picnic in the park (not on the grass), make a detour first to the old street-market behind the Panthéon,

After a tumultuous life, the Panthéon has found its vocation as a Mausoleum.

the bustling **Rue Mouffetard**. There, by the tiny Place de la Contrescarpe, old hunting ground of Rabelais and his spiritual descendants, you will find epicurean delights to fill your basket. Despite their 17th-century origins, the Luxembourg Gardens avoid the rigid geometry of the Tuileries and Versailles.

Back down by the Seine, but heading eastwards, stroll past the vast Jussieu University complex that stands on the site of the Halles aux Vins (wine market). The first **Institut du Monde Arabe** stands at 23 Quai Saint-Bernard (open 1 to 8pm, closed Sundays and Mondays), and was built with the help of 16 Arab nations. Its glass and aluminium façade pays homage to traditional Islamic architecture while remaining resolutely modern. Inside, a museum and library containing over 40,000 volumes cover all aspects of Muslim culture and studies.

For a change of scene, venture into the **Jardin des Plantes** next door. Louis XIII created the place as 'a royal **59**

one leg down in the water and its body spanning the main quayside road, is surprising to say the least – and gives people plenty to complain about.

MONTPARNASSE

Montparnasse is where they invented the cancan in 1845, at the now defunct Grande Chaumière dancehall. In the Twenties, it took over from Montmartre as the stomping ground of Paris's artistic colony, or at least its avant-garde, when Picasso moved over. Expatriates such as Hemingway, Gertrude Stein, F. Scott Fitzgerald and John Dos Passos also liked the free-living atmosphere and greatly added to the mystique themselves. Today, French and American tourists point out the places where the Lost Generation found themselves.

garden of medicinal plants'. After studying the small collection of cuddlies, creepy-crawlies and exotic plants in the hothouses, even the least scientifically minded will enjoy the rich and varied collections of the **Musée d'Histoire Naturelle**, with its armies of skeletons, but also butterflies and minerals, at last displayed to effect.

A tax office is never a popular sight, but the new **Ministère des Finances** on the other side of the Seine, with

SAINT-GERMAIN-DES-PRÉS

Saint-Germain-des-Prés isn't part of the Latin Quarter *per se*, but rather prolongs it. It's the literary quarter *par excellence*, home of the major publishing houses, intellectual cafés, Académie Française and bookshops to suit all tastes, as well as a charming neighbourhood that's great for people-watching. It was the headquarters of Jean-Paul Sartre and his existentialist acolytes, who wore, all winter and summer through, black corduroys and long woollen scarves.

Today, nightclubs have replaced the jazz cellars and existentialism has truly had its day, if that's not a contradiction in terms. But the easygoing atmosphere of the outdoor cafés still pervades the Place Saint-Germain-des-Prés. On the north side you'll find the Café Bonaparte and on the west the famous Café des Deux Magots. Both provide ring-side seats for the street theatre of mimes, musicians and fire-eaters, and for the neighbourhood eccentrics. The Café de Flore, just up the road, has hung on to its 'intellectual' tradition more than the others, perhaps because of its intense, ideologically confused history. It has been home successively to the extreme right-wing Action Française group under Charles Maurras in 1899, the Surrealists of Apollinaire and André Salmon in 1914 (they liked to provoke brawls), and then Sartre's existentialists, a peaceful bunch who never got enough sleep to have the energy to fight.

Saint-Germain also has its more formal monuments. The church of **Saint-Germain-des-Prés**, a mixture of Romanesque and Gothic styles restored last century, has a clock-tower dating back to around 1000. A 17th-century porch shelters 12th-century doorposts.

To the north of the square the Rue Bonaparte runs past the prestigious and rather pompous **Ecole des Beaux-Arts** (Fine Arts School). Incorporated in its structure are fragments of medieval and Renaissance architecture and sculpture that make it a living museum. More recently, in May 1968, it turned into a poster factory for the overnight creations of the students. **61**

The august **Palais de l'Institut de France**, home of the Académie Française, is on the Quai de Conti by the Pont des Arts. Designed by Louis le Vau in 1668 to harmonize with the Louvre across the river, the Institut began as a school for the sons of the provincial gentry, financed by a legacy of Cardinal Mazarin. In 1805 the building was turned over to the Institut, which comprises the Académie Française – the supreme arbiter of the French language founded by Riche-

Little Green Men

If cleanliness is next to godliness, then Paris is on its way to divinity. Jacques Chirac, Mayor of Paris, decided once and for all to make Paris not only beautiful but clean. He brought even dogs to heel, and forced them to use the gutters or dog 'toilets', as opposed to the pavements. One hundred specially equipped motorcycles were also introduced: their task is to clean up 1,600km (995 miles) of pavement divided up into 72 sectors. Some 30 inspectors prowl the capital, waiting to impose a hefty 600-franc fine on any dog owners found letting their dogs foul the pavement.

Chirac also brought in a green army, armed with great green brooms, which patrols the streets and pavements in green moon-exploration vehicles: 6,500 municipal workers wage a war on dirt, day in, day out, with a success rate envied by most other big cities. Some 525 great garbage trucks clatter around everyday at the crack of dawn, picking up household dustbins (in the chic *quartiers* this noisy business is done late in the afternoon). Strange green machines suck up anything that's left behind and hoses are used to freshen up the streets. Around 16,000 litter baskets, one every 150m, await the rubbish of some 3 million Parisians.

lieu in 1635 – and the Académie des Belles-Lettres, Sciences, Beaux-Arts and Sciences Morales et Politiques. The admission of a new member to the Académie Française is the occasion of a great ceremony. Guides to the Institut like to point out the east pavilion, site of the old 14th-century Tour de Nesle. They say that Queen Jeanne de Bourgogne used the tower to watch out for likely young lovers, whom she summoned for the night and then had thrown into the Seine.

Power and Grace

The **Palais-Bourbon**, seat of the National Assembly, provides a rather formidable riverside façade for the Left Bank's most stately district – the elegant 7th *arrondissement*, with its 18th-century embassies, ministries and noble residences (*hôtels particuliers*). The Grecian columns facing the Pont de la Concorde were added under Napoleon and belie the more graceful character of the Palais-Bourbon, as seen from its real entrance on the south side. Designed as a residence for a daughter of Louis XIV in 1722, this government building can be visited only on written request or as the guest of a deputy. If you do get in, look for the Delacroix paintings, illustrating the history of civilization, in the library.

If you are more interested in gracious living than supreme power, you will probably agree that it's better to be Prime Minister and live at the Hôtel Matignon than be President at the Elysée Palace. The Prime Minister's magnificent residence, at 57 Rue de Varenne, is just a short walk from the National Assembly. Its huge private park has a music pavilion much favoured for secret strategy sessions. The same tranquil street, a veritable museum of 18th-century elegance, contains the **Rodin Museum** in the Hôtel Biron (no. 77, closed Monday). You'll find the ever-moving statue of the *Thinker* in the garden. Inside, you'll not only discover Rodin the great sculptor but also the man.

63

LEFT BANK CHIC

(Invalides–Eiffel Tower)

From the quiet intimacy of Matignon, we return to the massively monumental with the **Hôtel des Invalides**. This was commissioned by Louis XIV, before the king set his heart on Versailles, and both château and hôtel were designed by the same architect, Jules Hardouin-Mansart. Picking up on an idea by Henri IV, Louis XIV founded the first national hospital for soldiers wounded in action. In Napoleon's hands, it also became an army museum. The Invalides came to symbolize the glory of Napoleon himself, when his body was brought back from St Helena for burial in the chapel.

The elaborate tomb is set directly under the Invalides' golden dome. It bears Napoleon's body, dressed in the green uniform of the Chasseurs de la Garde and encased in six coffins, Russian-doll fashion. The monument of red porphyry rests on a pedestal of green granite from the Vosges.

The church of **Saint-Louis-des-Invalides** is decorated with the flags taken by French armies in battle since Waterloo. At the entrance to the Invalides are two German Panther tanks captured by General Leclerc in the Vosges. The main courtyard contains the 18 cannons of the *batterie triomphale*, including eight taken from Vienna, which Napoleon ordered to be fired on momentous occasions – such as the birth of his son in 1811. The cannons sounded again for the Armistice of 1918 and the funeral of Maréchal Foch in 1929.

The military complex continues with the Ecole Militaire and the vast Champ de Mars, where officers have trained and performed military exercises since the middle of the 18th century.

In its heyday, 10,000 soldiers passed in review on this expansive parade ground. Horse races were held here in the 1780s and five World Fairs between 1867 and 1937. In the 20th century it has become a park for the Left Bank's most luxurious residences.

A Selection of Parisian Hotels and Restaurants

Recommended Hotels

Hotels in Paris range from the very expensive to the very reasonable. The following list is divided roughly into two sections: central Paris (*arrondissements* 1 to 8) and outer Paris (*arrondissements* 9 to 20). Within each category, the hotels are listed in alphabetical order and each entry is marked with a symbol indicating price range, per night, for a double room with bath but without breakfast. The Tourist Office in Paris – tel. (1) 49.52.53.54; fax (1) 49.52.53.00 – will provide a complete list on request.

Café-Couette, France's answer to the Bed & Breakfast system, provides affordable accommodation with the inhabitant. (Room with en suite bathroom for two persons: 390 F, breakfast included.) For further information, contact Café-Couette, 8 Rue de L'Isly, 75008 Paris. Tel. (1) 42.94.92.00; fax (1) 42.94.93.12

The hotels in this section have been chosen according to their price and location. They fall into one of three categories: luxury (anything above 1,750 F), medium-priced (between 800 and 1,750 F) and economic (below 700 F). You may find considerable variations on the spot, with perfectly acceptable rooms at 350 F. Many of the economic hotels have no restaurant. The last one or two figures of the postal code in each address indicates the *arrondissement* or district.

▌▌▌	above 1,750 F
▌▌	800–1,750 F
▌	below 800 F

CENTRAL PARIS

Abbaye Saint-Germain   ▌▌
10 Rue cassette, 75006
Tel. (1) 45.44.38.11

Fax (1) 45.48.07.86
42 rooms, 4 duplex. This ex-17th century abbey is situated between the Luxembourg Gardens and Saint-Germain-des-Prés. Friendly, attentive service.

Angleterre ‖‖

44 Rue Jacob, 75006
Tel. (1) 42.60.34.72
Fax (1) 42.60.16.93
27 rooms. A historic staircase leads to quality rooms. Patio for outdoor dining. Ernest Hemingway lived here.

Bristol ‖‖‖

112 Rue du Faubourg Saint-Honoré, 75008
Tel. (1) 42.66.91.45
Fax (1) 42.66.68.68
150 rooms, 45 apartments. The Bristol is a true palace. It comes complete with marble halls, antique furniture and garden, with the added bonus of a rooftop swimming pool.

Cayré ‖‖

4 Blvd Raspail, 75007
Tel. (1) 45.44.38.88
Fax (1) 45.44.98.13
125 rooms. Huge rooms. The hotel is much favoured by artists and writers.

Claridge Bellman ‖‖

37 Rue François-Ier, 75008
Tel. (1) 47.23.54.42
Fax (1) 47.23.08.84
42 rooms. In the chic district lying between the Seine and the Champs-Elysées. The *quartier* is devoted to the great names in French *couture*.

Concorde-St-Lazare ‖‖‖

108 Rue St-Lazare, 75008
Tel. (1) 40.08.44.44
Fax (1) 42.93.01.20
305 rooms. A true classic: the building is listed. Within easy reach of the Opéra, the major department stores, and St-Lazare station. *Terminus* restaurant.

Crillon ‖‖‖

10 Place de la Concorde, 75008
Tel. (1) 44.71.15.00
Fax (1) 44.71.15.02
120 rooms, 43 apartments. World-famous, hotel set right on the Place de la Concorde (the beautiful terrace dominates the *place*). Dream-like service and quality and two excellent restaurants: *Les Ambassadeurs* and *L'Obélisque*.

Des Deux-Iles ‖

59 Rue St-Louis en-l'Ile, 75004
Tel. (1) 43.26.13.35
Fax (1) 43.29.60.25
17 rooms. Set in a small and attractive mansion on the Ile Saint-Louis, this hotel is both comfortable and friendly. No restaurant.

Duc de Saint-Simon ‖‖

14 Rue de Saint-Simon, 75007
Tel. (1) 44.39.20.20
Fax (1) 45.48.68.25
29 rooms, 5 suites. At the very heart of the Faubourg Saint- **67**

Germain. This is an attractively furnished early 19th-century town house that seems to come straight out of a Balzac novel. Lovely private garden.

Duminy-Vendôme   ▌▌

3 Rue du Mont-Thabor, 75001
Tel. (1) 42.60.32.80
Fax (1) 42.96.07.83
79 rooms. A few steps from the Tuileries Gardens. Brass beds, flowery wallpaper and marble bathrooms in a homely setting. All modern amenities.

Edouard-VII   ▌▌

39 Avenue de l'Opéra, 75002
Tel. (1) 42.61.56.90
Fax (1) 42.61.47.73
76 rooms, 4 apartments. Large, airy rooms. *Delmonico* restaurant (closed August).

Hôtel de l'Elysée   ▌▌

12, Rue des Saussaies, 75008
Tel. (1) 42.65.29.25
Fax (1) 42.65.64.28
Near the Elysée palace, with good views and attractive décor.

Elysées-Maubourg   ▌▌

35 Blvd de la Tour-Maubourg,
  75007
Tel. (1) 45.56.10.78
Fax (1) 47.05.65.08
30 rooms, 1 appartment. Intimate atmosphere, friendly service, at-tractive décor and, comfortable rooms. On sunny days, the tiny interior courtyard is open and provides the ideal setting for afternoon tea.

France et Choiseul   ▌▌

239 Rue St. Honoré, 75001
Tel. (1) 42.61.54.60
Fax (1) 40.20.96.32
120 rooms. Central situation, ideal for the fashionable shops.

George-V   ▌▌▌

31 Avenue George V, 75008
Tel. (1) 47.23.54.00
Fax (1) 47.20.40.00
182 rooms, 39 apartments. This beautiful timeless hotel needs no introduction. It is situated just off the Champs-Elysées. Two Restaurants with French ambiance. Fine views from upper floors.

Henri IV   ▌

25 Place Dauphine, 75001
Tel. (1) 43.54.44.53
22 rooms. A modest hotel on the Ile de la Cité. Somewhat old-fashioned, but only a short walk from Notre-Dame and Saint-Michel.

L'Hôtel   ▌▌▌

13 Rue des Beaux-Arts, 75006
Tel. (1) 43.25.27.22
Fax (1) 43.25.64.81
25 rooms, each of them with a different décor, and 2 apartments.

Oscar Wilde died in one of them 'above his means'. Ideal location in the heart of the Saint-Germain-des-Prés area.

Inter-Continental   ▐ ▐ ▐

3 Rue de Castiglione, 75001
Tel. (1) 44.77.11.11
Fax (1) 44.77.14.60
375 rooms, 75 apartments. Modern amenities (including business centre) in a historic building designed by Charles Garnier, architect of the Opéra. *Café Tuileries* and *La Terrasse Fleurie* for outdoor dining.

Jeu de Paume   ▐ ▐

54 Rue St-Louis-en-l'Ile, 75004
Tel. (1) 43.26.14.18
Fax (1) 40.46.02.76
25 rooms, 7 duplex. Delightful situation, right at the heart of Paris. The hotel has kept its ancient, 17th-century '*jeu de paume*' court: a game that is said to be the predecessor of tennis. Great for a taste of old Paris.

Lancaster   ▐ ▐ ▐

7 Rue de Berri, 75008
Tel. (1) 40.76.40.76
Fax (1) 40.76.40.00
49 rooms, 10 apartments. An old town house, the *Lancaster* retains much charm. Thoughtful décor. Outdoor dining. Restaurant open for lunch only.

Lord Byron   ▐ ▐ ▐

5 Rue Chateaubriand, 75008
Tel. (1) 43.59.89.98
Fax (1) 42.89.46.04
25 rooms, 6 apartments. Close to the Etoile. Stylish decor and elegant courtyard.

Lotti   ▐ ▐ ▐

7 Rue de Castiglione, 75001
Tel. (1) 42.60.37.34
Fax (1) 40.15.93.56
133 rooms, 6 apartments. Under the arcades of the Rue de Castiglione, near the Tuileries Gardens: business people head for its restaurant at lunchtime. Elegant *fin de siècle* décor.

Lutèce   ▐ ▐

65 Rue St-Louis-en-l'Ile, 75004
Tel. (1) 43.26.23.52
Fax (1) 43.29.60.25
23 rooms. A small, charming hotel on the Ile Saint-Louis. The rooms on the 6th floor are certainly the most romantic. No restaurant.

Lutétia   ▐ ▐

45 Blvd Raspail, 75006
Tel. (1) 49.54.46.46
Fax (1) 49.54.46.00
271 rooms, 28 suites. One of the few old, traditional hotels on the Left Bank. Art-déco style décor makes for an elegant hotel that remains friendly. Restaurant, *Brasserie Lutétia*, piano bar.

69

Mayfair ▐▐
3 Rue Rouget-de-Lisle, 75001
Tel. (1) 42.60.38.14
Fax (1) 40.15.04.78
53 rooms. Very comfortable. No restaurant.

Plaza Athénée ▐▐▐
25 Avenue Montaigne, 75008
Tel. (1) 47.23.78.33
Fax (1) 47.20.20.70
211 rooms, 41 apartments. The absolute height of chic – also one of the most beautiful palaces in the world. Two restaurants.

Prince de Galles ▐▐▐
33 Avenue George-V, 75008
Tel. (1) 47.23.55.11
Fax (1) 47.20.96.92
169 rooms, 30 apartments. Restaurant *Le Jardin des Cygnes,* outdoor dining. On Sundays brunch only.

Relais Christine ▐▐▐
3 Rue Christine, 75006
Tel. (1) 43.26.71.80
Fax (1) 43.26.89.38
51 rooms, 10 duplex. Beautiful interior décor, lovely garden and courtyard. ▐ uiet situation.

Relais Medicis ▐▐
23 Rue Racine, 75006
Tel. (1) 43.26.00.60
Fax (1) 40.46.83.39
16 rooms. A tastefully decorated hotel, with oak-beamed rooms set around a quiet courtyard with fountain. Near the Odéon and Jardin du Luxembourg.

Résidence Maxim's de Paris ▐▐▐
42 Avenue Gabriel, 75008
Tel. (1) 45.61.96.33
Fax (1) 42.89.06.07
4 rooms, 33 suites. Luxury in a décor by Pierre Cardin. *L'atmosphère* restaurant.

Ritz ▐▐▐
15 Place Vendôme, 75001
Tel. (1) 42.60.38.30
Fax (1) 43.16.31.78
187 rooms, 42 apartments. A legend. *Ritz-Espadon* restaurant. Outdoor dining in beautiful terraced garden. Nightclub-cum-discothèque. Swimming pool, health club, squash court.

Royal Monceau ▐▐▐
37 Avenue Hoche, 75008
Tel. (1) 45.61.98.00
Fax (1) 42.99.89.90
219 rooms, 39 apartments. Swimming pool and fitness club. Outdoor dining. *Le Carpaccio* and *Le Jardin* restaurants, piano bar.

Saint-André-des-Arts ▐
66 Rue Saint-André-des-Arts, 75006
Tel. (1) 43.26.96.16
Fax (1) 43.29.73.34.

36 rooms. Lively atmosphere and very central position.

Saint Pères ▌▌
65 Rue des Saints-Pères, 75006
Tel. (1) 45.44.50.00
Fax (1) 45.44.90.83
39 rooms. ▌ uiet and comfortable. Modern, functional bedrooms. Favoured by the publishing world, who like to take breakfast in the small courtyard.

Le Tourville ▌
16 Avenue Tourville, 75007
Tel. (1) 47.05.62.62
Fax (1) 47.05.43.90
Good value accommodation, cosy, attractive decor. No restaurant.

OUTER PARIS

Baltimore ▌▌▌
88 bis, av. de Kléber, 75016
Tel. (1) 44.34.54.54
Fax (1) 44.34.54.44
105 rooms, 1 apartment. A vast, modern hotel, with all the comforts you would expect. A few minutes' walk from the Etoile. *Le Bertie's* restaurant with English cook from London's *Gavroche*.

Concorde La Fayette ▌▌▌
3 Place du Gén.-Koenig, 75017
Tel. (1) 40.68.50.68
Fax (1) 40.68.50.38

970 rooms, 16 suites. *L'Etoile d'Or*, *L'Arc-en-Ciel* restaurants. *Les Saisons* coffee shop. Panoramic bar on 33th floor.

Le Grand Hôtel ▌▌▌
Inter-Continental
2 Rue Scribe, 75009
Tel. (1) 40.07.31.00
Fax (1) 42.66.12.51
514 rooms, 48 apartments. A very grand hotel, with tasteful décor and good service. *La Verrière* garden restaurant. Beside the Opéra.

Hilton ▌▌▌
18 Avenue Suffren, 75015
Tel. (1) 42.73.92.00
Fax (1) 47.83.62.66
455 rooms, 36 apartments. *La Terrasse* and *Le Western* restaurants.

Le Laumière ▌
4 Rue Petit, 75019
Tel. (1) 42.06.10.77
Fax (1) 42.06.72.50
54 rooms. Excellent value-for-money hotel, with modern, comfortable rooms. A little out of the way, but very popular.

Magellan ▌
17 Rue J.-B. Dumas, 75017
Tel. (1) 45.72.44.51
Fax (1) 40.68.90.36
75 rooms. Comfortable hotel in a quiet location. Garden. Well placed for La Défense.

Méridien ▯ ▯ ▯

81 Blvd. Gouvion-St-Cyr, 75017
Tel. (1) 40.68.34.34
Fax (1) 40.68.31.31
1025 rooms, 23 suites. Near the Paris Convention Centre, and therefore much favoured by business people. *Le Clos Longchamp*, *Le Café l'Arlequin* and *Le Yamato* (Japanese) restaurants, jazz club.

Nikko ▯ ▯ ▯

61 Quai de Grenelle, 75015
Tel. (1) 40.58.20.00
Fax (1) 45.75.42.35
779 rooms, 6 apartments. View over the Pont Mirabeau. Indoor swimming pool. *Les Célébrités*, Brasserie *Pont Mirabeau* and *Le Benkay* Japanese restaurant.

Regent's Garden ▯ ▯

6 Rue P.-Demours, 75017
Tel. (1) 45.74.07.30
Fax (1) 40.55.01.42
39 rooms. ▯ uiet situation. Attractive garden.

Sofitel Paris
Porte de Sèvres ▯ ▯ ▯

8–12 Rue L.-Armand, 75015
Tel. (1) 40.60.30.30
Fax (1) 45.57.04.22
539 rooms, 14 apartments. Panoramic bar and indoor swimming pool on the 23rd floor. Restaurant and *La Tonnelle* brasserie. Popular with business people.

Splendid Étoile ▯ ▯

1 Avenue Carnot, 75017
Tel. (1) 45.72.72.00
Fax (1) 45.72.72.01
57 rooms. View across to the Arc de Triomphe. *Le Pré Carré* restaurant.

Terrass' Hotel ▯ ▯

12 Rue J.-de-Maistre, 75018
Tel. (1) 46.06.72.85
Fax (1) 42.52.29.11
101 rooms, 13 suites. Indoor restaurant and *La Terrasse* roof-top restaurant open May to September, piano bar.

AIRPORTS

Hilton Orly ▯ ▯

94544 Val-de-Marne
Tel. (1) 45.12.45.12
Fax (1) 45.12.45.00
359 rooms. Near airport and railway station. View. *La Terrasse* restaurant. Free transport to the airport.

Holiday Inn ▯ ▯

1 Allée du Verger, 95700
Roissy-en France.
Tel. (1) 34.29.30.00
Fax (1) 34.29.90.52
243 rooms. All the comforts you would expect from this well-known hotel chain. Good restaurant. Free transport to the airport.

Recommended Restaurants

The restaurants are divided, again, into two rough categories: central Paris (arrondissements 1 to 8) and outer Paris (arrondissements 9 to 20). They are further divided by price, where luxury refers here to 600 F-plus for a full meal and a reasonable wine, medium-priced to 400–600 F and lower-priced to 400 F and under – which again doesn't rule out the multitude of restaurants with excellent menus at around 150–200 F, and even less for a fixed menu at lunchtime. The following list is by no means exhaustive, but does contain establishments noted for the quality of their cuisine.

Many restaurants close in August, and advance booking is always recommended.

▌▌▌ above 600 F

▌▌ 400–600 F

▌ below 400 F

CENTRAL PARIS

Les Ambassadeurs ▌▌▌
10 Place de la Concorde, 75008
Tel. (1) 44.71.15.00
18th-century setting. *Les Ambassadeurs* is open every day, all year round. Outdoor dining. Modern cuisine, without any excesses.

Ambroisie ▌▌▌
9 Place des Vosges, 75004
Tel. (1) 42.78.51.45
Closed Sunday and Monday. This aristocratic mansion in the grandiose setting of the Place des Vosges offers a refined modern cuisine based on traditional recipes.

Benoît ▌▌
20 Rue St.-Martin, 75004
Tel. (1) 42.72.25.76
The Benoît is a popular place and you need to book two or three days in advance. Traditional *cuisine bourgeoise* in a real bistrot that has barely changed since its foundation in 1912. Open every day.

Gérard Besson ▮ ▮

5 Rue du Coq-Héron, 75001
Tel. (1) 42.33.14.74
Much respected for its fish (imported from the Côtes d'Armor) and poultry dishes. Closed Saturday evening and Sunday.

Bistrot de Paris ▮

33 Rue de Lille, 75007
Tel. (1) 42.61.16.83
1900-style bistro, with a lovely billiard room on the first floor. Owner Michel Olivier (a TV chef) lives up to his excellent reputation. Closed Saturday lunchtime and Sunday. Book well ahead.

Le Bourdonnais ▮

113 Avenue de la Bourdonnais,
75007
Tel. (1) 47.05.47.96
A friendly atmosphere in this little restaurant serving both traditional and sophisticated food.

Bristol ▮ ▮ ▮

112 Rue du Faubourg St.-Honoré,
75008
Tel. (1) 42.66.91.45
The restaurant of the very grand Hôtel Bristol. Delightful garden in summer and Régence woodwork décor in winter.

Bûcherie ▮ ▮

41 Rue de la Bûcherie, 75005
Tel. (1) 43.54.78.06
Wonderful situation right opposite Notre-Dame Cathedral. *Nouvelle cuisine* predominates. Friendly service.

Jacques Cagna ▮ ▮ ▮

14 Rue des Grands-Augustins,
75006
Tel. (1) 43.26.49.39
Fax (1) 43.54.54.48
Set on the first floor of an old Parisian mansion, with sturdy beams in the ceiling and still lifes on the walls. Closed Saturday lunchtime and Sunday. Book ahead for a table in the evening.

Carré des Feuillants ▮ ▮

14 Rue de Castiglione, 75001
Tel. (1) 42.86.82.82
Fax (1) 42.86.07.71
Book two days ahead. Excellent cuisine, with a distinct flavour of the south-west (Armagnac). A luxurious décor with contemporary still lifes. Closed Saturday lunchtime and Sunday.

Le Céladon ▮ ▮

15 Rue Daunou, 75002
Tel. (1) 42.61.57.46
Fax (1) 42.60.30.66
In the hôtel Westminster. More frequented at lunchtime than in the evening, this elegant and excellent restaurant offers a light, modern, subtle cuisine. Closed Saturday and Sunday.

Chez Françoise

Aérogare des Invalides, 75007
Tel. (1) 47.05.49.03
Chez Françoise is a favourite rendez-vous for French Parliamentarians. The restaurant specializes in smoked meat and fish.

Chez Omar

47 Rue de Bretagne, 75003
Tel. (1) 42.72.36.26
Excellent couscous and grills at this popular Tunisian restaurant. Lively atmosphere in the evening. Closed Sunday lunchtime.

Chez Pauline

5 Rue Villedon, 75001
Tel. (1) 42.96.20.70
More than 'just' a bistrot: a treat with plenty of new ideas. Game in season and specialities such as *queues de langoustine en bouillabaisse*. Closed Saturday and Sunday.

Chiberta

3 Rue Arsène-Houssaye, 75008
Tel. (1) 45.63.77.90
Very faithful clientèle at this popular, tasteful restaurant just beside the Etoile. Closed Saturday, Sunday and holidays.

Copenhague

142 Avenue des Champs-Elysées, 75008
Tel. (1) 43.59.20.41

Situated near the Etoile. The restaurant's lovely patio injects some country air. Danish specialities.

Le Divellec

107 Rue de l'Université, 75007
Tel. (1) 45.51.91.96
Fax (1) 45.51.31.75
Seafood. Closed Sunday. First-rate restaurant, particularly strong on fish; simple but succulent dishes.

Duquesnoy

6 Avenue Bosquet, 75007
Tel. (1) 47.05.96.78
Fax (1) 44.18.90.57
Closed Saturday lunchtime and Sunday. A recent facelift has also the cuisine – most innovative. Try, for instance, a *Saint-Jacques fumé à la minute*.

La Fermette Marbeuf

5 Rue Marbeuf, 75008
Tel. (1) 47.20.63.53
Worth a visit for the Art Nouveau setting in the back room, with ceramics and cast-iron columns – as well as for the food.

La Flamberge

12 Avenue Rapp, 75007
Tel. (1) 47.05.91.37
Excellent cuisine in this discreet restaurant. We recommend the game in season. Closed Saturday lunchtime and Sunday.

75

Grand Véfour ▯▯▯

17 Rue de Beaujolais, 75001
Tel. (1) 42.96.56.27
Fax (1) 42.86.80.71
Late 18th-century establishment in the Palais-Royal setting. Closed Saturday and Sunday. Light, modern cuisine.

Lipp (Brasserie) ▯▯

152 Blvd Saint-Germain, 75006
Tel. (1) 45.48.53.91
Everyone who's anyone in Saint-Germain-des-Prés has a table here. Not to be missed for a view of the neighbourhood eccentrics.

Lucas-Carton ▯▯▯

9 Place de la Madeleine, 75008
Tel. (1) 42.65.22.90
Fax (1) 42.65.06.23
Beside the Madeleine. Brilliantly original cuisine by Alain Senderens. Closed Saturday lunchtime and Sunday.

Mercure Galant ▯▯

15 Rue des Petits-Champs, 75001
Tel. (1) 42.96.98.89
Fax (1) 42.96.08.89
A large, old-fashioned, 19th-century style restaurant. Excellent cuisine. Closed Saturday lunchtime and Sunday.

Miraville ▯

72 Quai Hôtel de Ville, 75004
76 *Tel. (1) 42.74.72.22*

A much appreciated restaurant just beside the Hôtel de Ville, with reasonable prices. Closed Saturday lunchtime and Sunday.

Au Pied de Cochon ▯▯

6 Rue Coquillière, 75001
Tel. (1) 42.36.11.75
Cheerful restaurant, open 24 hours every day. Specialities are fish and pigs' trotters stuffed with truffle pâté. In the Les Halles *quartier*.

Pharamond ▯

24 Rue Grande-Truanderie, 75001
Tel. (1) 42.33.06.72
In an authentic Belle Epoque setting, a restaurant that turns the lowliest offal and giblets into divine dishes. Closed Sunday and Monday lunchtime.

Perraudin ▯

157 Rue Saint-Jacques, 75005
Tel. (1) 46.33.15.75
Bourgeois cuisine in the Latin uarter: *andouillette*, beef bourguignon and *tarte Tatin*, all served with a smile. Closed Saturday and Monday lunchtime and Sunday.

Récamier ▯▯

4 Rue Récamier, 75007
Tel. (1) 45.48.86.58
Fax (1) 42.22.84.76
Publishers and politicians rub shoulders and enjoy the first-rate,

hearty cuisine. Closed Saturday lunchtime and Sunday.

Régence ▯ ▯ ▯

25 Avenue Montaigne, 75008
Tel. (1) 47 23 78 33
In the Hôtel Plaza-Athénée. Perhaps the most sumptuous of all Parisian 'palaces'.

Relais Louis XIII ▯ ▯

1 Rue du Pont de Lodi, 75006
Tel. (1) 43.26.75.96
Historical house, with an atmosphere to go with it. Traditional cuisine with modern touches. Fish gets best treatment. Closed Sunday and Monday lunchtime.

Restaurant d'Alsace ▯

39 Avenue des Champs-Elysées
75008
Tel. (1) 43.59.44.24
Open 24 hours a day for great Alsatian specialities. A popular place on the Champs-Elysées.

Ritz-Espadon ▯ ▯ ▯

15 Place Vendôme, 75001
Tel. (1) 42.60.38.30
Grandiose setting of real old-style 'palace'. Outdoor dining.

Taillevent ▯ ▯ ▯

15 Rue Lamennais, 75008
Tel. (1) 45.61.12.90
An extremely well known and appreciated restaurant. Book at least two months ahead for dinner. Beautiful former *hôtel particulier*. Closed Saturday and Sunday

Tan Dinh ▯

60 Rue Verneuil, 75007
Tel. (1) 45.44.04.84
Popular venue, and arguably the best Vietnamese cuisine in town. Closed Sunday.

Le Texan ▯

3 Rue Saint-Philippe du Roule,
75008
Tel. (1) 42.25.09.88
Fashionable décor and some of the best Tex-Mex food in town. Closed Saturday lunchtime and Sunday.

Tour d'Argent ▯ ▯ ▯

15–17, Quai de la Tournelle,
75005
Tel. (1) 43.54.23.31
Lovely view of Notre-Dame. In the cellars, over 300,000 bottles make up an historical wine exhibit. Book at least a month in advance. Closed Monday.

Jules Verne ▯ ▯

2nd floor, Eiffel Tower, 75007
Tel. (1) 45.55.61.44
Fax (1) 47.05.94.40
Reserve well in advance. Exciting décor by Slavik. Good view of Paris overlooking the Palais de Chaillot.

OUTER PARIS

Amphyclés ▯▯
78 Avenue des Ternes, 75017
Tel. (1) 40.68.01.01
Fax (1) 40.68.91.88
Small restaurant serving excellent cuisine at a reasonable price, with warm, friendly service. Closed Saturday lunchtime and Sunday.

Apicius ▯▯
122 Avenue de Villiers, 75017
Tel. (1) 43.80.19.66
Fax (1) 44.40.09.57
Often considered to serve one of the best meals in Paris, this restaurant has become very popular. Excellent from beginning to end. Closed Saturday and Sunday.

Beauvilliers ▯▯
52 Rue Lamarck, 75018
Tel. (1) 42.54.54.42
Fax (1) 42.62.70.30
Unusual décor. Terrace with outdoor dining. Closed Monday lunchtime, Sunday and public holidays.

Le Bistrot d'André ▯
232 Rue Saint-Charles, 75015
Tel. (1) 45.57.89.14
This used to be the local bistrot for the workers of André Citroën's car factory; it used to belong to the great man himself. Entirely decorated with old documents, it's the perfect setting for traditional French cooking, such as beef bourguignon. Closed Sunday.

Le Café Moderne ▯
19 Rue Keller, 75011
Tel. (1) 47.00.53.62
A young team in an old bistrot offers heart-warming traditional cuisine, such as black pudding and Morteau sausage, as well as lighter fare, like salmon tartare. Closed Sunday.

La Cagouille ▯
*10 Place Constantin-Brancusi,
  75014*
Tel. (1) 43.22.09.01
Fax (1) 45.38.57.29
Very popular restaurant, famous among fish-lovers for its simple, quality dishes and fresh ingredients. Modern décor. Set in the Montparnasse *quartier*.

Les Célébrités ▯▯▯
61 Quai de Grenelle, 75015
Tel. (1) 40.58.20.00
In the Hôtel Nikko. An elegant setting with excellent service.

Charlot Ier 'Merveilles des Mers' ▯▯
128 bis Blvd de Clichy, 75018
Tel. (1) 45.22.47.08
Just beside Place Clichy. Fish specialists. Remarkably well but simply prepared fish – and as fresh

as can be. One of the best places in Paris to try a *bouillabaisse*. Open every day.

Chartier
7 Rue du Faubourg Montmartre, 75009
Tel. (1) 47.70.86.29
This is one of the least expensive meals in town, attracting hordes for its low prices and charming old-fashioned décor. Good, traditional French cuisine, though not a gourmet's paradise.

Au Chateaubriant
23 Rue de Chabrol, 75010
Tel. (1) 48.24.58.94
The French poet Jacques Prévert used to be a regular, and the décor lends the restaurant an 'artistic' feel. Good wine list. Closed Sunday and Monday.

Conti
72 Rue Lauriston, 75116
Tel. (1) 47.27.74.67
The chef, formerly with the Troisgros brothers in Roanne, is particularly noted for working wonders with pasta. Closed Saturday, Sunday and public holidays.

Etoile d'Or
3 Place du Général-Koenig, 75017
Tel. (1) 40.68.51.28
Fax (1) 40.68.50.43
In the Hôtel Concorde-Lafayette. In spite of its size, the *Etoile d'Or* is a most welcoming restaurant, with excellent service and cuisine. Closed Saturday lunchtime and Sunday.

Faugeron
52 Rue de Longchamp, 75116
Tel. (1) 47.04.24.53
Fax (1) 47.55.62.90
The customer is treated like royalty in this pleasant restaurant. Distinctive yellow and blue décor. One of the best wine waiters in Paris will help you with the wine list. Saturday lunchtime and Sunday.

Guyvonne
14 Rue de Thann, 75017
Tel. (1) 42.27.25.43
Guy Cros likes to cook fish, and you can choose from six or seven different kinds on the menu, depending on arrivals. Offal and country fare are also worth noting. Closed Saturday and Sunday.

Le Madigan
22 Rue de la Terrasse, 75017
Tel. (1) 42.27.31.51
High-class food, especially fish and crustaceans fresh from the tank. And for dessert, the Madigan offers a nightly recital of music, with reputed performers. Closed Sunday.

79

Le Manoir de Paris ‖ ‖
6 Rue Pierre-Demours, 75017
Tel. (1) 45.72.25.25
Delightful Belle Epoque setting and contemporary cuisine. Upstairs, *La Niçoise* serves delicious Provençal dishes in a much lower price range. Closed Saturday lunchtime and Sunday.

Morot-Gaudry ‖ ‖
6 Rue de la Cavalerie, 75015
Tel. (1) 45.67.06.85
Rooftop dining with splendid view. Classical but original cuisine. Closed Saturday and Sunday.

Opéra-Café de ‖ ‖
la Paix
Place de l'Opéra, 75009
Tel. (1) 40.07.30.10
Fax (1) 40.07.33.75
A fine setting for the authentic traditional cuisine. Closed Saturday and Sunday.

Le Pré Catelan ‖ ‖
Route de Suresnes, 75016
Tel. (1) 45.24.55.58
Fax (1) 45.24.43.25
Beautiful surroundings in the Bois de Boulogne with abundant greenery. Excellent seasonal menu.

Relais d'Auteuil ‖ ‖
31 Blvd Murat, 75016
Tel. (1) 46.51.09.54
Fax (1) 40.71.05.03
A youthful and inspired cuisine. Try the *menu dégustation* for an idea of the chef's range. Closed Saturday lunchtime and Sunday.

Michel Rostang ‖ ‖ ‖
20 Rue Rennequin, 75017
Tel. (1) 47.63.40.77
Fax (1) 47.63.82.75
Book well in advance. Welcoming atmosphere in modern setting; impeccable fresh produce. Closed Saturday lunchtime and Sunday.

Sormani ‖ ‖
4 Rue du Gén.-Lanrezac, 75017
Tel. (1) 43.80.13.91
Italian cuisine in the grand manner, with an excellent wine list. Closed Saturday and Sunday.

Timgad ‖
21 Rue Brunel, 75017
Tel. (1) 45.74.23.70
Fax (1) 40.68.76.46
North African cuisine in a comfortable setting. Attentive service. If you are in a group, try the *méchoui* – lamb roast on a wood fire.

Vivarois ‖ ‖ ‖
192 Avenue Victor-Hugo, 75116
Tel. (1) 45.04.04.31
Fax (1) 45.03.09.84
Claude Peyrot's cuisine is splendidly inventive; try the warm or cold terrines and pâtés. Closed Saturday and Sunday

Right from the start, the **Eiffel Tower** was a resounding success. In 1889, 2 million visitors paid 5 francs a head to climb to the top, and the figures have shown consistently that, whatever its critics may have said, the Tower has its rightful place in the Parisian landscape.

Some monuments celebrate heroes, commemorate victories, honour kings or saints. The Eiffel Tower, on the contrary, is a monument for its own sake, a proud gesture to the world, a witty structure that makes aesthetics irrelevant. Its construction for the World Fair of 1889 was an astounding engineering achievement – 15,000 pieces of metal joined together by 2,500,000 rivets, soaring 320m (984ft) into the sky on a base of only 130sq m (1,400sq ft). Forty tonnes of paint were required to spruce it up; 10,000 gas lamps lit it up at night. At the time, the Eiffel Tower was the tallest structure in the world. It also provided the perfect perch for the then new radio aerial.

On its inauguration, the lifts weren't yet operating and Prime Minister Pierre-Emanuel Tirard, aged 62, stopped at the first platform (57m or 187ft high), leaving his Minister of Commerce to go all the way up to the top to present Gustave Eiffel with the Legion of Honour medal. The tower (that 'hollow chandelier', as Huysmans called it) had been conceived as a temporary structure for the Fair and was slated for destruction in 1910. But nobody had the heart to go through with it. Today it would be a sacrilege to touch it (no one is even suggesting it) and in late 1985, when new spotlights were installed to illuminate the tower from *within*, even its detractors had to admit that it did have something.

There is a restaurant on the first platform, and bars on the second and third. From the top platform on a pollution-free day, the eye stretches for about 65km (40 miles) – but often you get a clearer view from the second. Try to get there one hour before sunset for the best view. **81**

Major Museums

Paris boasts more museums than any other capital and their number is growing by the day. Entrance fees can be high, especially if you have a whole family to pay for. So if you intend to make the most of the city's museums, look into the very advantageous Museum Pass (see p.132). On Sundays some museums are free or half-price, and many museums close on Tuesday.

THE GRAND LOUVRE

Pride of place obviously goes to the Louvre, far less daunting and stuffy since its facelift and the addition of the Pyramide, but formidable by its sheer size. Don't let yourself be put off – it's actually an exhilarating experience to come to grips with the world's most comprehensive museum of painting and sculpture, with artefacts from 5000 BC to 1848, date at which the Musée d'Orsay takes over).

Perhaps the best way to tackle the museum is to spend a morning going round the highlights, then another day making a beeline for your particular interests. Acoustiguides (50-minute recorded tours available in six languages) are very helpful.

Don't neglect the outside of the museum – its harmonious lines are particularly striking now that the ambitious new works and cleaning of the Richelieu wing (the former Ministry of Finance) are underway. It's deceptive: the Louvre has been eight centuries in the making, beginning with Philippe Auguste's fort in 1190 in the eastern Cour Carrée (designed to protect Paris from fluvial attack while he was away on a crusade), to François Mitterrand's great glass Pyramide of the 1980s in the Cour Napoléon. Get up very early one sunny morning and walk across the gardens of the Place du Carrousel. Admire Maillol's sensual statues and sit on a bench to take in the immensity of this home of France's kings and monumental showcase of the world's treasures.

83

The 'new' Louvre has been further expanded by the removal of the Finance Ministry from the north wing on Rue de Rivoli (see p.60), and it is brilliantly organized. Essentially, it is divided into three 'regions', each named after one of France's great men: the Richelieu wing (due to open in 1993), the Sully wing in the east, and Denon running alongside the Seine. Each 'region' is then divided into numbered '*arrondissements*',

and each floor colour-coded. The ground floor is blue, the first floor is red and the second yellow. The mezzanine floor, where the earliest remains of Philippe Auguste's fort have been found, is grey.

Whatever you might think of it, the latest addition to the Louvre, the Pyramide designed by Chinese-American I. M. Pei, provides a spectacular modern entrance. You descend by escalator into the bowels of the earth, complete

with ticket office, underground bookshops and cafés, from where corridors lead to the various wings of the museum.

As for the contents of the museum, by 1793 when the leaders of the Revolution declared the palace a national museum, there were 630 works of art in the collection; at the most recent inventory there were 250,000. So it's as well to establish a clear list of priorities. For an overall view of the collections (the 'highlights tour'), we've attempted our own selection:

Egyptian: the lion-headed goddess *Sekhmet* (1400 BC) and the colossal *Amenophis IV* (1370 BC).

Greek: the winged *Victory of Samothrace* and beautifully proportioned *Vénus de Milo*.

Italian: the splendid sculpture of the *Two Slaves* by Michaelangelo; Leonardo da

The Louvre old and new. Paris's most famous museum benefits from the addition of I. M. Pei's glass Pyramid.

Vinci's fabled *Mona Lisa* (*La Joconde*), and also his sublime *Virgin of the Rocks*; Titian's voluptuous *Woman at her Toilet* and the sombre *Entombment of Christ*; the poignant *Old Man and His Grandson* by Ghirlandaio.

French: Poussin's bittersweet *Arcadian Shepherds*; Watteau's hypnotically melancholy *Gilles* and his graceful *Embarkation for Cythera*; Fragonard's erotic *Le Verrou* (*The Bolt*), Delacroix's *Liberty Guiding the People* and Courbet's piercing study of provincial bourgeoisie, *Funeral at Ornans*.

Dutch and Flemish: Rembrandt's cheerful *Self-Portrait with a Toque*, his beloved *Hendrickje Stoffels*, also portrayed nude in *Bathesheba Bathing*; Van Dyke's gracious dignified *Charles I* of England; among scores of 'official' Rubens, his tender *Helena Fourment;* Jordaens' *Four Evangelists* as diligent Dutchmen.

German: a gripping *Self-Portrait* by Dürer; Holbein's *Erasmus*.

85

Spanish: the uncompromising Velázquez portrait of the ugly *Queen Marianna of Austria*; El Greco's powerfully mystic *Christ on the Cross*; Ribera's gruesomely good-humoured *The Club Foot* (*Le Pied-Bot*).

English: Gainsborough's exquisite *Conversation in a Park*; Turner's *Landscape with River and Bay*.

American: Whistler's *Mother*.

ORSAY

'The station is superb and truly looks like a Fine Arts Museum, and since the Fine Arts Museum resembles a station, I suggest ... we make the change while we still can,' wrote the painter Edouard Detaille in 1900, with a touch of irony. In 1986 that was more or less what happened. Facing the Tuileries across the river, the converted 19th-century hotel-cum-railway station has been transformed into the huge and impressive **Musée d'Orsay**, devoted to French works of art between 1848 and 1914. In effect, it carries on where the Louvre leaves off. Keeping the exterior much as it was, Italian interior architect Gae Aulenti conceived the museum to group under one roof the scattered works of that period. The

*L*eft: Delacroix's Liberty Guiding the People, in the Louvre. Below and right: sculpture is well represented in the Musée d'Orsay.

wide-ranging artistic activity of the mid-19th and early-20th centuries – not least the magnificent Impressionist collections formerly held in the Jeu de Paume – has found the perfect niche in the Musée d'Orsay. Sculpture is well represented, as are all other art forms; photography is present from its inception (1839).

Both layout and lighting are astonishing, and every inch of the ex-railway station has been used in an imaginative way. Plenty of lectures, guided tours and concerts also animate the magnificent buildings. Opening times are from 10 a.m. to 6 p.m. (Thurdays to 9.45 p.m), closed Monday.

BEAUBOURG

'That'll get them screaming,' said Georges Pompidou as he approved the plans (chosen from 681 projects) for the Centre National de l'Art Contemporain, better known as Centre Pompidou or, shorter still, as Beaubourg – after the 13th-century neighbourhood surrounding it.

How right he was: controversy raged for years over this multicoloured 'oil refinery', while the building imperceptibly became, like the Eiffel Tower, part of the Parisian landscape. The combination of public library, modern art museum, children's workshop and special library, cinémathèque, industrial design centre, experimental music laboratory and open-air circus on the front plaza, the parvis, is a permanent hive of activity and one of the most popular shows in town.

The comparison with an oil refinery is readily accepted by the Centre Pompidou's architects, Italians Renzo Piano and Gianfranco Franchi, and Englishman Richard Rogers, who deliberately left the building's service system visible. Some 11,000sq m (1,18400sq ft) of glass, 15,000 tonnes of steel, no less than 30 air-conditioning stations and 41 escalators make up the structure that is 42m high and 166m long (135 by 543ft).

The construction statistics are pretty astonishing, as is

the centre's cultural 'record' of 700 exhibitions, 1,000 debates and lectures, and 600 concerts in 15 years. Ninety million visitors have been to Beaubourg since its opening in 1977.

If the paint is peeling and some of the initial glamour has faded, there's more activity going on than you can fit in a day's outing. Watch the entertainers on the *parvis*, sit by the wild Tinguely sculptures at the Fontaine Stravinsky or take the escalators that run diagonally from the bottom

*B*eaubourg's parvis *is one of the most animated spots in the city.*

left to the top right-hand corner and watch Paris unfold before your eyes (the thrilling rooftop view of the skyline is best seen between the third and fourth floors, not the fifth).

CITÉ DES SCIENCES ET DE L'INDUSTRIE: LA VILLETTE

If there's one thing this institution dislikes, it's being called a museum. First, the Cité harbours a whole range of museums and activities,

and second, it favours a hands-on philosophy that puts the accent on participation. But as with any good museum, you learn a great deal and enjoy yourself even more.

The trip to La Villette (on the tatty, north-eastern fringe of town, metro Porte de la Villette) means a day well spent for those who want to come to grips with the world of science. Architect Alain Fainsilber plays on three themes (water, light and vegetation) and two colours (blue and

grey). The unabashed functionalism of its architecture takes the Beaubourg principle to its logical conclusion – and La Villette is four times bigger. A user-friendly approach will delight all visitors, while even the most scientifically minded won't fail to appreciate the high quality of the information presented.

Its most attractive symbol is the shining stainless-steel **Géode** sphere, made up of 6,433 triangles of stainless steel, housing a revolutionary cinema with a hemispheric screen 36m (118ft) in diameter. As you watch the film, you feel as if you were part of it. There's also a giant rock-concert hall, the **Zénith** and since it's set in a park and beside a canal (you can reach it by boat from central Paris, see p.118), it's very much a family outing.

La Villette's most startling landmark, the Géode sphere, harbours a revolutionary cinema screen.

Day Trips

VERSAILLES

Anyone who dubs himself 'the Sun King' has to be mightily conceited. Louis XIV was quite simply a megalomaniac; luckily he also had wit, taste and an extraordinary vision. He was wary of Paris and its rabble (all too easily roused) and rising aristocracy (ever-demanding and arrogant). What better way to keep potential trouble-makers under his thumb than to coop up the whole lot at Versailles, and let them jostle for position or squabble for rights and privileges as futile as attending the His Majesty's awakening?

Never did a piece of architecture express so well the personality of its builder. Versailles is magnificently excessive and as extravagant, pompous, dazzling, formidable and vainglorious as the man himself. If Louis XIII had hoped to turn his favourite hunting ground into a modest retirement home, his son and **91** heir made it the centre of a universe, proclaiming his own grandeur in an edifice of brick, marble, gilt and crystal.

A visit of the château, a most popular excursion from Paris, is an easy day trip, just 21km (13 miles) from the capital. But to do Versailles justice, you'll need a full day and an early start. You can take the RER (line C5), or go on one of the organized bus tours that leave from the Tuileries Gardens on the Rue de Rivoli side. However, given its size, you may prefer to 'do' things in your own time. One suggested itinerary includes a morning tour of the palace; a stroll through the gardens for lunch beside the Grand Canal (a packed lunch is in order to avoid Versailles' tourist traps); then a siesta and tea in the gardens of the Petit Trianon; finally, wander back across the palace gardens for a last view of the château at sunset. (Note that it is closed on Mondays.)

The central part of the building, where the royal family lived, was conceived in 1661 by Louis Le Vau (whom we've already met in the Marais and elsewhere), Jules Hardouin-Mansart and landscape designer André Le Nôtre. It was completed 21 years later. Le Vau also designed the marble courtyard, decorated with 84 marble busts. Inside, past the grand gates, the rooms not to be missed are: the **Royal Chapel**, a gem of high Baroque, where the king could keep an eye on how pious his courtiers were; the **Grands Appartements** where the king entertained his courtiers three times a week (or vice versa); the **Salon de Diane**, where Louis would try his hand at billiards – since it didn't go down too well to beat a Sun King, he always won; finally (after many sumptuous rooms) you reach the glittering **Galerie des Glaces**, 73m (240ft) long and built to catch every ray of the setting sun in the 17 tall, arched panels of mirrors. In the **Queen's bedroom**, 19 royal children were

92

*T*he splendour of Versailles and its formal gardens never fail to impress.

born, the births often attended by members of the public, as was the custom. Louis XV's superb royal **opera** and the **King's bedroom**, where he died of gangrene of the leg in 1715, are usually part of a separate visit.

The most impressive façade is the west one, facing the gardens; try to be there at 3.30 p.m. when the fountains begin to play (three Sundays a month, from May to September). You should also see the Grand Trianon, the little palace that Louis XIV used to get away from the château, the Petit Trianon favoured by Louis XV, and the lovely Hameau or 'cottage' where Marie-Antoinette went to get away from everything.

LA DÉFENSE

An excursion, La Défense? Though part of Paris, it stands on the very fringes of the capital, and its peripheral status is much emphasized by the Parisians. At the end of the long Avenue de la Grande-Armée leaving from the Etoile, the battery of towers grows bigger and bigger as you approach through the chic, leafy suburb of Neuilly, in the 16th *arrondissement*. Cross the river and there you are: in a concrete jungle that has somehow managed to get a soul.

An international business district La Défense may be, but that's not its only prerogative. After May 1968 President Pompidou, trying to modernize France, started this mini-Manhattan that has grown by fits and starts till recently, and become a city within the city.

The **Grande Arche** looms up from a distance beyond the towers, but only when you get closer to it do you realize that it is far, far bigger than you ever imagined – and further away than you thought. A huge hollow cube 110m high and 106m across (360 by 347ft), it's wide enough for the Champs-Elysées to pass through it and tall enough for Notre-Dame cathedral, lock, stock and barrel, to fit beneath it. Built at a remarkable speed by Danish architect, Johann-Otto von Sprekelsen (he won the contest in

94

1983 and it was ready in 1989), the Grande Arche lies directly in line with the Louvre's Cour Carrée, but on a slight bias with the Champs-Elysées. If you approach from Paris or the west, the white gables you'll see are clothed in Carrara marble and the external façades with smooth grey marble and glass. The inside walls are covered with aluminium.

From the foot of the steps on the vast *parvis* (forecourt), the sheer scale of the Arche takes on an awesome quality. The two 'legs' contain offices, while the roof houses four conference rooms and several patios – home to Jean-Pierre Reynaud's *Carte du ciel* (map of the sky). Bubble lifts whoosh you up to the terrace through the fibreglass and Teflon 'cloud', floating on a web of pure steel cables that stretch from one wall to the other.

*T*he complex of La Défense has been dubbed a 'mini Manhattan' and a 'city within the city'. Judge for yourself.

Take a lunch break in the company of Miró and Calder's giant works or beside a 'crazy' Tinguely fountain. The 36 statues, fountains and murals by celebrated modern artists, all detailed on special street-plans, are evenly scattered around the 11 sectors of the Défense complex, which extends from the Arche down into tiered terraces to the broad main alley and on to the Pont de Neuilly.

DISNEYLAND PARIS

Disneyland Paris merits more than just a day trip. It offers a comprehensive holiday centre with multiple attractions and facilities for a stay of several days. Besides the theme park there is an artificial lake, an entertainment centre, a championship-size golf course, tennis courts, swimming pools, hotels, camping facilities, restaurants and a convention centre. For further information, ring 64 74 30 00.

The resort is located at Marne-la-Vallée, some 32km (20 miles) east of Paris. A motorway (*autoroute*) provides easy access from both the capital and the international airports of Roissy (Charles-De-Gaulle) and Orly. Rapid commuter trains (RER) from Paris and high-speed long-distance trains (TGV) from the provinces drop off visitors just outside the entrance to the Theme Park.

The Theme Park is divided up into five 'lands' – Frontierland, Adventureland, Fantasyland and Discoveryland – all leading off from Main Street, USA, a land all to itself.

Recapturing the traditions of small-town America, Main Street is the starting point for the park's activities. Here you will see the ice-cream parlours of America's 20th-century childhood. Dad can get an old-fashioned shave and a short-back-and-sides haircut, while the rest of the family is serenaded by a quartet of crooners. A Statue of Liberty tableau is an apt reminder that the New York monument was actually a gift from France in the 1880s.

The voyage into past and future gets into full swing with the tour of the four 'lands' bordering on Main Street, USA. **Frontierland** captures the pioneering atmosphere of an American mining town and the Wild West, complete with ranch, shooting gallery and Indian canoes. The big attraction of **Adventureland** is a sail on the high seas with the Pirates of the Caribbean, or you can explore caves, tunnels and waterfalls on Adventure Island. **Fantasyland** draws more directly on the fun of

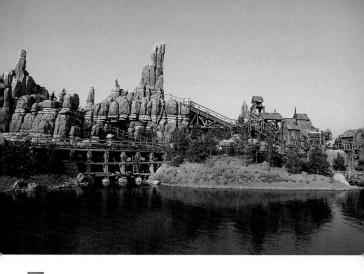

*E*njoy the thrills and spills of Big Thunder Mountain.

Walt Disney's classic cartoon films. The major focus is Sleeping Beauty's towering castle (the Château de la Belle au Bois Dormant), or you can meet Pinochio, Peter Pan, Dumbo and many other familiar characters. From the fairytale past of Fantasyland, **Discoveryland** whisks you back to the present and beyond it to the future. You can ride in a spaceship at Orbitron, a modern sports car at Autopia, take a trip through space on Starspeeder at Star Tours, or join Michael Jackson in a 3-D movie at CinéMagique.

Everywhere you go, you'll see hosts Mickey, Minnie, Goofy, Donald Duck and Pluto wandering around in their familiar costumes, happy to pose with visitors.

What to Do

For the day-to-day breakdown of what's on where in Paris, you'll need to buy the excellent weekly entertainment guides, *Pariscope* or *l'Officiel des Spectacles*. A clear and handy companion to this travel guide is the Berlitz *Paris Address Book*, which lists about 1,000 indispensible addresses covering a variety of topics.

SHOPPING
Some Pointers

Most shops and department stores are open from 8 or more often 9 a.m. till 7 p.m., Tuesday to Saturday. Some shops close at lunchtime, from noon till 2 p.m, and many are closed on Monday mornings, if not all day Monday. Bakeries are the first to open their doors, and there's always a small grocer's (*épicerie*) where you can get everything till 9 or even 10 in the evening in summer. On Sundays, too, you are never stuck, even if food shops tend to close at midday. The Drugstore on the Champs-Elysées

*S*hopping underneath the arcades of the Place des Vosges.

is open till 12 every night. The battle over Sunday openings is still raging.

Stores and Shops

You may like to set aside a day or two for shopping and group your purchases (in this way non-EU residents may be able to benefit from duty-free allowances). You need to buy over 2,000 FF of goods from a single store to claim duty-free allowances (though the sum can be made up of various items). EU residents cannot claim refunds on duty.

The **department stores** best equipped to deal with foreign visitors are the Galeries Lafayette and Le Printemps, next-door neighbours on the Boulevard Haussmann. In both, staff is at hand to help non-French-speaking clients. They will explain how to fill the *bordereau* (the export sales

invoice) and reclaim VAT (TVA). The Galeries has lost its great central staircase of old but the circular galeries still provide the most startling décor of Paris's big stores. The chinaware department is enormous and the perfume and luggage sections excellent. Le Printemps, next door, has the biggest-ever selection of shoes and is famous for its lingerie and vast toy department.

The **FNAC** belongs to the younger generation of Parisian department stores. Branches at the Etoile, Montparnasse and the Forum des Halles, as well as la Défense, stock the city's largest selection of **books**, **CDs** and discount records, as well as **cameras**, hi fi, **electronics** and sports goods. Virgin Megastore, on the Champs-Elysées, completes the FNAC on a merely musical note. Other department stores, such as Marks & Spencers and C&A, have branches in Paris, but more typical French department stores are Au Bon Marché at Sèvres-Babylone and the Samaritaine at the Pont-Neuf, where you'll find everything from home furnishings to pets. It also offers a splendid view of the city from its 10th-floor bar.

An extraordinary collection of **art books** is now available at the bookshop below the **99**

Pyramide du Louvre. The Centre Pompidou bookshop isn't bad either.

As for **fashion and accessories**, Paris remains paramount, despite worthy competition from Rome, Tokyo and elsewhere. From the Right Bank around the Rue du Faubourg-Saint-Honoré, the Avenues Montaigne and George-V and over to the Halles and Place des Victoires, the *haute couture* houses and their ready-to-wear boutiques have spilled over to the Left Bank, around Saint-Germain-des-Prés.

For **leather goods**, Hermès (on Rue du Faubourg Saint-Honoré) is an institution in its own right, catering to the tastes of the horsey set and men-and-women-about-town, with high-quality handbags, luggage, stirrups and boots right up to the ultimate diary and address book. On Avenue Montaigne, Louis Vuitton's luggage needs no introduction.

The young favour a great variety of shops – chain stores such as Dorothée Bis, Naf Naf, Pimky, Benetton, etc. Another

French speciality is **children's clothes**, though you may baulk at the prices. Try chains like Jacadi or Tartine et Chocolat. Cheaper but of lower quality is the Tati chain (the branch at Barbès-Rochechouart is particularly well known, but be prepared to jostle).

Good Buys

Antiques. Let's face it, there's virtually no chance of picking up a treasure that has slipped through the hands of the experts, but it's fun to have a try. Many of the stands at the **flea markets** are manned by professional antique dealers. The Marché aux Puces of Saint-Ouen at the Porte de Clignancourt groups half a dozen of them.

A far cry from these popular haunts are the high-priced **antique shops**, grouped mainly in the Left Bank shops of Paris's 6th and 7th *arrondissements*. The Carré des Antiquaires, a little rectangle bounded by the Quai Voltaire and the Boulevard Saint-Germain, and the Rues du Bac

Try your hand at bargain hunting, for the best souvenir of Paris.

and des Saints-Pères, constitutes a veritable museum of ancient Egyptian, Chinese, pre-Columbian, African and Polynesian art, as well as Louis XV, Second Empire, Art Nouveau and Art Déco. The biggest concentration of antique dealers in Europe (some 250) is at the Louvre des Antiquaires, 2 Place du Palais-Royal, closed on Monday.

Modern Art lovers will find galleries galore in the Boulevard Saint-Germain and the streets off it.

The **book trade** (old and new) flourishes particularly well on the Left Bank, in or round the Latin Quarter, in particular at the Odéon. The second-hand booksellers, better known as **bouquinistes**, line the quays of the Seine, especially between Pont Saint-Michel and Pont des Arts. It's worth rummaging through the mass of books, postcards and periodicals for the occasional find. If you're pining for English-language books, there's Brentano's in the Avenue de l'Opéra, W. H. Smith on the Rue de Rivoli, or the NQL at the top of Boulevard Saint-Michel.

Household goods tend to be rather cumbersome to take home, but kitchenware is of particularly high quality. The old food-market district of Les Halles has held on to its restaurant supply shops, offering an astonishing array of pots and pans, kitchen knives and other utensils at the venerable Dehillerin in the Rue Coquillière, and Mora in the Rue Montmartre.

Gourmet delicacies make wonderful presents to take home with you. Thanks to new packaging methods, it's usually possible to transport goods that previously spoiled *en route* and many stores are equipped to export your purchases for you. The two most

famous luxury grocery shops, Fauchon and Hédiard, glare at each other across the Place de la Madeleine.

As for **wine**, the best bargains in Paris are at the Nicolas chain stores, with 150 branches in Paris alone. The greatest selection is at Legrand, Rue de la Banque (bankers and stockbrokers are notorious connaisseurs). The most intriguing wineshop is perhaps the Caves de la Madeleine, Rue Boissy d'Anglas, where an Englishman holds wine-tasting sessions.

Strong **liqueurs** may be less expensive at the duty-free shops but the choice will be more limited.

SPORTS

The fitness craze has caught on in France: everybody is looking for ways of keeping fit, slim and beautiful. Simplest is *le jogging* or *le footing*, which takes place mostly in the big parks of the Bois de Boulogne and Bois de Vincennes, though there's also plenty going on in the Tuileries and even round Concorde. More challenging

are the hilly Parc Montsouris (on the Left Bank) or Buttes-Chaumont (on the Right). Also popular is Left Bank of the Seine between the Pont-Neuf and Pont-Royal.

As an alternative to jogging you can discover Paris by bike. Call (1) 45.38.58.58 for information on bike tours of the city or surrounding areas such as Versailles.

There are several public courts where you can play **tennis**: contact the Fédération Française de Tennis (Stade Roland Garros, 2 Av. Gordon-Bennett), or resort to the jungle law of first-come-first-serve at the Luxembourg Gardens public courts. As for clubs, Paris boasts over 400, to which some hotels have access for their guests.

As many as 30 municipal pools are available for **swimming** in Paris. The most serious action takes place at the Olympic-size indoor pool of the Centre de Natation, at 34 Boulevard Carnot.

As far as spectator sports are concerned, pride of place goes to **horse racing**. Longchamp's 'Arc de Triomphe' and Auteuil in summer are the most important international events of the horse racing calendar, every bit as elegant as Britain's Ascot. The serious punter who wants to avoid the frills and champagne can have a very good time at Vincennes, at the trotting races.

Football and **rugby** can be seen at the modern stadium of Parc-des-Princes; **tennis tournaments** take place at Roland-Garros. (Both stadiums are in the Bois de Boulogne.) The Palais Omnisports de Paris-Bercy, beside the Gare de Lyon, was designed for a variety of sports and houses everything from rock concerts to tango competitions, as well as cycling races. **103**

ENTERTAINMENT

Nearly a century ago, Paris had a reputation for glitter and bounce – a reputation that has sustained itself over the centuries. The Moulin Rouge (Place Blanche) still puts on one of the great boisterous **floor shows** of Europe, in the old tradition. The rest of Pigalle is sleazy indeed, but then it always was.

Taste may have changed over the years, but Pigalle has always managed to plumb its lower depths with a certain glee that continues to exert an almost anthropological fascination for visitors. Except for one or two shows with talented transvestite imitators, there's very little on the artistic front happening round here, though plenty of a dubious nature. Two noteworthy exceptions among music halls: the Folies Bergères (Rue Richer), which launched the careers of Josephine Baker, Mistinguett and Maurice Chevalier, still survives, and the Casino de Paris (Rue de Clichy) carries on seemingly eternally.

Over on the Champs-Elysées the Lido, another classic among classics, continues to attract crowds with very professional shows of Bluebell girls in fishnet stockings and little else. Perhaps the most famous modern-day floorshow, conceived with great

*P*igalle cultivates its 'gay Paree' image, whilst new areas, such as Bastille, develop their own style of entertainment.

choreographic talent and in which the girls are dressed only in cunning patterns of light, is at the Crazy Horse Saloon (Avenue George-V). On the Left Bank, two shows combine pretty girls and pretty transvestites in a non-stop riot of pastiche and satire: the Alcazar in the Rue Mazarine and the Paradis Latin in the Rue du Cardinal-Lemoine.

Suppose you'd rather do the **dancing** yourself; there's a plethora of **nightclubs** to choose from. Keeping up with the latest *boîte* is a full-time job for the professional night-owl. Broadly speaking, the expensive and exclusive Paris discos hide out around the Champs-Elysées, notably in the Rue de Ponthieu and the Avenue Matignon, while the younger crowds haunt ear-drum-busters around Les Halles. The area round Bastille (Rue de Lappe) is popular too.

The French take their **jazz** very seriously, and Paris boasts 15 jazz clubs. The New Morning (Rue des Petites Ecuries) attracts all the major American and European mu-

sicians, while Le Dunois (Rue Dunois) is an intimate place, cultivating the avant-garde.

Pop and rock concerts are held at the spectacular new Zénith in the Cité de la Musique (La Villette, metro Porte de Pantin). However, it's perhaps in the realm of **classical music** that Paris has come into its own. The recently opened Opéra-Bastille may **105**

have attracted some criticism for its architecture, but its acoustics have received nothing but praise. The National Opera has set up house there, and the seats are reasonably priced. The Opéra-Garnier is the seat of the National Ballet Company, but will be closed for refurbishment for most of 1995. All ballets will be transferred to the Opéra-Bastille.

Modern dance is enjoying a revival, with a new wave of small, imaginative companies starting off modestly at the Café de la Danse (Passage Louis-Philippe), Théâtre Garnier and Centre Pompidou, before reaching the great heights of the Théâtre de la Bastille.

Classical **theatre** maintains its exacting standards for the plays of Molière, Racine or Corneille at the Comédie Française (Rue de Richelieu). Even with minimum French, playgoers can enjoy the innovative contemporary theatre found at the Bouffes du Nord (Boulevard de la Chapelle), suburban Théâtre des Amandiers (Nanterre) and Cartoucherie de Vincennes (Avenue de la Pyramide). Drawing-room comedies (*comédies de boulevard*) find long-running homes in the theatres around the *grands boulevards*.

One French national pastime is the **cinema**, with 300 different films showing every week in the capital. You'll find

*M*usic fans will love the Opéra de Paris-Bastille.

*T*ake time to relax in the Jardin du Luxembourg.

at least one cinema showing films in V.O., an undubbed version with French subtitles.

Paris doesn't really go in for **celebrating** national or religious holidays in grand style, but for the Bastille Day celebrations on 14 July you can still find a *bal populaire* in the Marais or the younger quarters of the city, or enjoy the traditional fireworks at Trocadéro.

Finally, the most enjoyable evening entertainment (and also the cheapest) is people-watching. For this purpose the Bastille, the Champs-Elysées, Beaubourg and Les Halles come into their own, while Saint-Germain-des-Prés and the Latin Quarter (more traditional haunts) are still good fun. A little coffee can go a surprisingly long way.

Eating Out

The scene changes, but there's never a doubt: Paris is the nirvana of any gourmet. Some tourists come to Paris, never set foot in a church nor a museum and wouldn't dream of 'wasting' their time shopping, and yet come away with tales of adventure, excitement, poetry and romance – and the feeling they know the city inside out. They have spent their time indulging in epicurian delights, with a nap between meals.

If your stomach (or the bill) won't allow it more than once, then give yourself *one* occasion to remember.

A Meal in a Nutshell

It's a shame to forego the starter (*hors d'œuvre)* – simple dishes, such as *crudités*, melon and *charcuterie* genuinely whet the appetite, and doing without this appetizer will not speed up service, if you're in a hurry. A dish of *crudités* can consist of raw vegetables – green pepper, tomatoes, celery, cucumber or just radishes by themselves – served with salt and butter. Salads are traditionally served as a separate course between the meat and the cheese but come more and more in the form of starters.

Fish comes fresh to Paris every day. Trout is delicious *au bleu* (poached absolutely fresh), *meunière* (salted in butter), or *aux amandes* (sautéed with almonds). Sole and turbot take on a new meaning when served with *sauce hollandaise*, that miraculous, smooth emulsion of egg yolks, butter and lemon juice with which the

Dutch have only the flimsiest connection.

For your main meat dish, you'll expect it to be less well done than in most countries – extra rare is *bleu*, whilst rare is *saignant*, medium *à point* and well done *bien cuit*. Steaks (*entrecôtes* or *tournedos*) are often served with a wine sauce (*marchand de vin* or *bordelaise*) or with shallots (*aux échalotes*).

General de Gaulle once asked how one could possibly govern a country with over 400 cheeses. Just about all of them find their way to Paris and a wide selection is often offered. On a *plateau de fromages* (more and more you are served little portions rather than being left to help yourself), try a variety: perhaps a hard (*pâte dure*) and soft (*pâte molle*) one, or a strong-tasting blue cheese (*bleu*), if possible a Roquefort, or a Brie de Meaux or *fromage de chèvre* (goat's cheese) and a milder Port Salut or Roblochon.

Indulge in a dessert and you won't be disappointed. Usually on offer are heavenly *mousse aux chocolat*, *profiteroles*, gâteaux or tarts (*aux pommes*, *poires*, *abricots* or whatever fruit is going). Don't miss the *Tarte Tatin*, made of hot caramelized apples.

There should be house wines (*réserve du patron*) at affordable prices; a wine list with only grand names can turn a reasonable meal into an expensive one. House wines are perfectly acceptable, even good. Wines in a carafe are served by the quarter (*quart*) or half (*demi*) litre.

Coffee (unless you specify otherwise) is a small cup of black coffee. Note that in a café you pay more sitting at a table than at the counter. Tea is usually awful. For a beer, ask for a '*demi*' (unless you want a bottle).

France on Your Plate

You will find all these cuisines and more in Paris.

Burgundy, the historic cradle of French culinary art, is ideal for those with a robust appetite. This wine-growing region produces the world's **109**

greatest beef stew, *bœuf bour-guignon*, beef simmered in red wine for at least four hours with mushrooms, small white onions and chunks of bacon. Its Bresse poultry is considered France's finest and the Charolais beef provides the tenderest of steaks. Why not give snails (*escargots*) a try? Start with a half-dozen and you may find the chewy texture of snails and the garlic sauce addictive.

Lyon, the gastronomic capital of France, is renowned for the quality of its pork, wild game, vegetables and fruit.

Onion soup (*soupe à l'oignon*) is a local invention; and *à la lyonnaise* generally means sautéed in onions. Dishes include (for starters), *cœurs d'artichaut* (artichoke hearts), *foie gras*, or *gratin de queues d'écrevisses* (baked crayfish tails). More standard is the *saucisson de Lyon*.

Brittany is celebrated chiefly for its seafood, served fresh and unadorned on a bed of crushed ice and seaweed. Brittany's *plateau de fruits de mer* is unbeatable; it will often include oysters (*huîtres*), clams (*palourdes, praires*), mussels (*moules*), scallops (*coquilles Saint-Jacques*), large prawns (*langoustines*), periwinkles (*bigorneaux*) that you winkle out with a pin, large whelks (*bulots*), and chewy ablones (*orneaux*) and whatever else the sea has turned up that day. Purists prefer their lobster (*homard*) grilled or steamed.

Normandy makes full use of its prolific dairy farms. Cream and butter are staples of the cuisine. The *caneton à la rouennaise* (duckling with a spicy red-wine sauce thickened with minced duck livers) comes from Rouen, while the local apples (*Reinette*) turn up with flambéed partridge (*perdreau flambé aux reinettes*) and in *poulet au Calvados* (chicken with apple-brandy sauce). Besides Camembert cheese, sample the stronger Livarot or the Pont-l'Evêque.

Bordeaux is the second wine-growing region in France and is also justly famous for its *bordelaise* sauce, made with white or red wine, shallots and beef marrow, served variously with *entre-*côte steaks, *cèpe* mushrooms or (why not?) with lamprey eels (*lamproie*).

Provence marries Mediterranean seafood with garlic, olives, tomatoes and the country's most fragrant herbs. For starters, try fresh grilled sardines with just a sprinkle of lemon juice for a taste of the south. Or spicy *tapenade*, an olive and anchovy paste that is delicious on toast. *Daube de bœuf* (beef stew with tomatoes and olives) is excellent, as is the celebrated *bouillabaisse*, a fish soup.

Landes, **Languedoc**, **Périgord** are famous for truffles and *pâté de foie gras* (goose-liver pâté), and for all the rich goose and duck dishes, especially *confit d'oie* and *confit de canard*.

Paris Abroad

As befits a thoroughly cosmopolitan capital, open to new ideas even where cuisine – a French preserve – is concerned, Paris has welcomed ethnic restaurants. The original trickle has become a flood, **111** and there are more types of restaurant in the capital than there are nations at the UN.

The French themselves have taken to ethnic restaurants, and they provide a very satisfactory alternative to a solid diet of French food. As a variation on the ubiquitous Chinese restaurants – many of them now quite luxurious establishments around the Champs-Elysées and Les Halles – try the Vietnamese, Laotian and Cambodian places in the Latin Quarter and the 13th *arrondissement*, behind the Place d'Italie. Since the flux of 'Boat People' in the 70s, the 13th quarter has become a haven for south-east Asians. Their cuisine uses distinctive touches of mint, lemon-grass (*citronelle*) and ginger, and a great variety of seafood. Thai restaurants, serving more highly spiced food, are growing in popularity, as are Japanese restaurants.

Rue Saint-Séverin has become a centre for Greek and Tunisian restaurants, but for a more 'genuine' Maghrebin atmosphere, it's become fashionable to head for the suburb of Belleville, home to a sizeable community.

Indian food is also making great headway in its assault on the Parisian palate, going beyond simple curries and tandoori to the grander subtleties of the Mughal and Kashmiri cuisines.

Wine Lore

French wine waiters (*sommeliers*) are there to help, not to terrorize you, and are happy to show off their knowledge if you express interest and ask their advice. Ordering a bottle of wine has far fewer rules than you think. If you happen to prefer red to white, you can safely order red with fish; a light, chilled Beaujolais (Morgon or Brouilly) goes well with both fish and meat. And if you are partial to white, you can drink dry burgundy with fish and wine from Alsace with everything, in all impunity. You prefer beer? Go ahead, it goes very well with Toulouse sausage and Alsatian *choucroute* (sauerkraut).

But if you do want to know more, here are a few basic pointers. The burgundy reds divide easily into two categories: those that can more safely be drunk relatively young (the supple Côte de Beaune wines of Aloxe-Corton, Pommard and Volnay), and those that need to age a little (the full-bodied Côte-de-Nuits wines of Vougeot, Gevrey-Chambertin and Chambolle-Musigny. The great names for burgundy whites include both Meursault and Puligny-Montrachet.

Bordeaux wines have four main regional divisons: Médoc, an aromatic, mellow red with a slight edge to it; Graves, a soft, easy-to-drink red, both dry and vigorous; Saint-Emilion, dark, strong and full-bodied; and the pale golden Sauternes, sweet and fragrant, the most distinctive of the soft aromatic wines. The lesser Bordeaux can be drunk when a couple of years old but the good ones need five years.

The Loire Valley produces fine dry white wines, such as Vouvray and Sancerre, and robust reds like Bourgueil and Chinon. Perhaps the best known red wine outside Bordeaux and Burgundy is the Châteauneuf-du-Pape, originating from the Rhône Valley and truly magnificent when mature.

And for a sparkling finish, don't forget the nation's pride and joy from that little area east of Paris, between Reims and Epernay: Champagne, which they describe as '*aimable, fin et élégant*' (friendly, refined and elegant). That's one way of putting it.

BLUEPRINT
for a
Perfect Trip

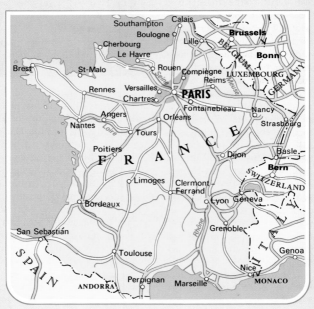

An A–Z Summary of Practical Information

Listed after most main entries is an appropriate French translation, usually in the singular. You'll find this vocabulary useful when asking for information or assistance.

ACCOMMODATION (see also RECOMMENDED HOTELS & RESTAURANTS, YOUTH HOSTELS and AIRPORTS)

Paris offers a wide range of hotels to suit every possible taste and wallet. The city is an extremely popular destination all year round, however, so that booking in advance is highly recommended. Be warned: during the holiday seasons (spread out throughout the year) and commercial fairs (*salons*), Paris is taken by storm and rooms are almost impossible to find.

Officially, hotels are classified into five categories; a complete booklet is available from the Paris Tourist Information Office (see pp.140–1). Rates are fixed according to the hotel's amenities and location, and posted visibly at reception desks and in every bedroom.

For a longer stay you might consider renting. Most national newspapers carry advertisements and, on the spot, *Le Figaro* and the *International Herald Tribune* also list accommodation for rent.

Do you have a single/double room for tonight?	**Avez-vous une chambre pour une/deux personnes pour cette nuit?**
with bath/shower/toilet	**avec bains/douche/toilettes**
What's the rate per night?	**Quel est le prix pour une nuit?**
I'm looking for a flat to rent for a month.	**Je cherche un appartement à louer pour un mois.**

AIRPORTS (aéroport)

Paris has two main airports. Roissy-Charles-de-Gaulle is about 25km (15 miles) north-east of the city and has two terminals (CDG 1 deals with most international flights; CDG 2 deals essentially with Air France flights). Orly is about 15km (9 miles) to the south, with its two buildings, Orly-Sud and Orly-Ouest. Most intercontinental flights use Charles-de-Gaulle, a space-age, modular construction. Both airports have currency exchange banks, excellent restaurants, snack-bars, post offices and duty-free shops.

There is a regular and comfortable bus service between the two main airports and between the airports and Paris. The buses leave frequently from about 6 a.m. to 11 p.m. The terminals (aérogare) for Charles-de-Gaulle airport are at Porte Maillot, near the Etoile, and at Opéra; you can also board the bus at the Arc de Triomphe (Avenue Carnot). Orly is served by the Invalides terminal and by the Orlybus (departing every 15 minutes from the Denfert-Rochereau RER station). The journey from Denfert to Orly takes about 25 minutes. The same applies going in the opposite direction, with buses leaving from both south and west terminals. Average time from Porte Maillot to Roissy and from the Invalides to Orly is around 40 minutes, depending on traffic. In normal conditions, it takes about an hour and a quarter to get from one airport to the other by bus, but you should leave early during peak traffic hours. Taxis are plentiful, but there's an extra charge for taking it from the airport (see p.134).

Trains leave every 15 minutes from about 5 a.m. to 11 p.m. and take 45 minutes to an hour and a quarter from the Gare du Nord to Charles-de-Gaulle. From the Quai d'Orsay, Austerlitz or Saint-Michel stations to Orly, the trip takes 40 to 60 minutes and trains leave frequently from early morning to late at night. Orly is now linked by RER (line B) to Paris by Orlyval (the journey takes 19 minutes; departure every day, every 7½ minutes on average, more at peak hours). You just need to change at Anthony (opposite platform, a few steps away).

There is also a regular helicopter service between airports and Paris. The Héliport de Paris is at 4 Avenue de la Porte de Sèvres, in the south-west (metro Balard).

Hotel reservations can be done at the arrival halls. At CDG 1 go to Porte 36, where a desk is open from 7.30 a.m. to 11 p.m. There, you can book hotels, shows, etc. (A deposit of 12% is required, which will be deducted from the bill.) Alternatively, use the electronic notice board next to the desk. This system enables you to contact (free of charge) a wide range of hotels throughout the city. You will find similar amenities in CDG 2's terminals. For any further gneral information, call the Renseignements Généraux service on (1) 48.62.22.80. (Charles-de-Gaulle) or (1) 49.75.15.15. (Orly). Language shouldn't be a problem, as most staff speak English.

BOAT TRIPS

If you love boats (and even if you don't), treat yourself to a daytime trip up or down the Seine at the beginning of your stay, or to a romantic night-time cruise at the end to enjoy the illuminations. Multilingual commentaries bring the river cruises to life. Times vary, but they usually start running from about 10 a.m. to about 10.30 p.m.

Parisians themselves have taken to the waters, and find their **Bat-O-Bus** with its five key-stops a very convenient way of travelling, traffic-jam-free, in a west–east direction. Stops are at Eiffel Tower (quai de la Bourdonnais), Musée d'Orsay (port de Solferino), Louvre (quai Malaquais), Notre-Dame (quai de Montebello), Hôtel de Ville (quai de l'Hôtel de Ville).

The **bateaux-mouches** – low-lying, glass-fronted boats, have open-air and covered seating. The standard hour-long tour starts at the Pont de l'Alma going west to the Pont Mirabeau and turning back upriver to the Pont Sully at the far end of the Ile Saint-Louis. You can also take lunch or dinner on board the restaurant boats (from 12 to 14.45 p.m. Saturdays and Sundays only, and from 8 p.m. to 10.45 p.m. every day) – a rather smart affair, since anoraks and blue-jeans are frowned upon and jacket and tie are *de rigueur*. Meals should be booked in advance; tel. (1) 42.25.96.10.

The **vedette** or motorboat tours take 60 minutes. The Vedettes Paris Tour-Eiffel depart from the Pont d'Iéna (Left Bank) and the Quai de Montebello, going west to the Pont Bir-Hakeim and east to the Pont Sully and back. They run from 10a.m. to 6 p.m. in winter, until 9.30 p.m. at weekends, and until 11 p.m. in summer. For information tel. (1) 44.11.33.44.

The **Vedettes du Pont-Neuf** leave from the Pont-Neuf, Square du Vert-Galant to the Eiffel Tower and back around the islands. Night cruises run from 1 May to 15 October from 9 p.m. to 10.30 p.m. (departure every 30 minutes). Tel. (1) 46.33.98.38.

The **Patache Eautobus** offers half-day cruises to the Parc de la Villette, north-east of the city, via the Seine and the Canal Saint-Marti, departing from the musée d'Orsay at 9.30 a.m. and from Parc de la Villette at 2.30 p.m. (April to November only). The bigger **Canotier** offers a one-day guided cruise up the Seine and the Marne to Champigny, boarding at the Musée d'Orsay. Prior booking is essential; ring (1) 42.40.96.97. Also runs weekends and holidays.

C

CAR HIRE (*location de voitures*)
Local firms may offer lower prices than international companies, but the latter will often let you return the car at any branch in the country, at no extra cost. Ask for any available seasonal deals.

To hire a car, you must show your driving licence (held for at least one year) and a passport. The minimum age for hiring cars ranges from 20 to 23. A substantial deposit is usually required – unless you hold a credit card recognized by the car-hire company – and you'll be asked for proof of your hotel or local address. The deposit is refundable. Third-party insurance is compulsory. Refer to the Yellow Pages (*Pages Jaunes*) for details, under *Location de voitures*.

I'd like to hire a car now/ tomorrow.	**Je voudrais louer une voiture tout de suite/ demain.**
118 for one day/a week	**pour une journée/une semaine**

CHILDREN

From dawn to dusk, with few exceptions, the activities that interest you are, fortunately, likely to interest children, too. The Eiffel Tower and boat trips are good fun for everyone. Paris's main zoo, open daily from 9 a.m. to 5.30 p.m., is in the Bois de Vincennes and can be reached easily by metro (Porte Dorée station). The Jardin d'Acclimatation of the Bois de Boulogne is a very special games-and-zoo park, complete with pony rides, puppet shows and other attractions. Prices are reasonable and children love it. The Jardin is open from 10 a.m. to 6 p.m. every day. Tots will find puppet shows and pony rides in the Jardin du Luxembourg, where they may also enjoy watching the toy boats capsize in the fountain. A raft of activities goes on at the Centre Pompidou, including art workshops on Wednesday and Saturday afternoons (tel. (1) 44.78.40.36); ask for the Atelier des Enfants. For the scientifically minded, there's a great deal to learn and a lot more to enjoy at the Cité des Sciences et de l'Industrie at La Villette. Some 30km (20 miles) outside Paris at Marne-la-Vallée, the Disneyland Paris Resort has enough to keep children happy for days ... or weeks. From Roissy-Charles-de-Gaulle, take the A104 then the A4 towards Marne-la-Vallée, or take the eastern line of the RER (A4, Torcy) till the Marne-la-Vallée–Chessy station. For more information on this popular destination, refer to the Berlitz Travel Guide.

It would be a shame not to go the restaurant in Paris, but children may not feel so enthusiastic at the prospect of a long formal meal. Order *à la carte* for them or take the '*Menu Enfants*', if available.

CLIMATE

Paris enjoys a mild Continental climate without extremes of hot or cold. From mid-July to the end of August there seem to be more tourists than French people around in Paris and many restaurant-owners pack up themselves and go off on holiday, curtailing the choice of establishment. In most respects, the best seasons to visit Paris are spring and autumn, though winter is perfectly bearable and summer temperatures are pleasant in the main.

The following chart will give you an idea of the temperatures you're most likely to meet:

	J	F	M	A	M	J	J	A	S	O	N	D
°C	3	4	7	10	14	16	19	18	15	11	6	4
°F	37	39	45	50	57	61	66	64	59	52	43	39

COMPLAINTS

If you do have a complaint to make, do it on the spot, calmly, and to the correct person. At the hotel or restaurant, ask to speak to the manager (*maître d'hôtel* or *directeur*). In extreme cases, a police station *(commissariat de police)* may help or, failing that, outside Paris, try the regional administration offices (the *préfecture* or *sous-préfecture*). Ask for the *service du tourisme*. If you have good reason to complain, a firm manner, a sense of humour and a little French are your most useful assets.

I'd like to make a complaint.   **J'ai une réclamation à faire.**

CRIME (*délit*)

Keep items of value in your hotel safe and obtain a receipt for them. It's a good idea to leave large amounts of money there as well. Travelling late on the metro and even the bus isn't recommended, though the risks are the same in any big city.

   Never leave a car unlocked, and if possible remove the radio-cassette player. Don't leave anything in view, especially in car parks: lock them in the boot. Any loss, theft or attempt at breaking into your car should be reported immediately to the nearest *commissariat de police*. A report will help back home with the insurance claim.

CUSTOMS (*douane*) & ENTRY FORMALITIES

Nationals of EU countries and Switzerland need only a valid passport to enter France. Nationals from Canada, New Zealand and the USA require valid travel documents whilst Australian and South

African nationals must get hold of a visa. For the latest information on entry requirements, contact the French embassy in your country.

The following chart shows the main items you may take into France and, when returning home, into your own country:

Into:	Cigarettes		Cigars		Tobacco	Spirits		Wine
France 1)	200	or	50	or	250g	1L	and	2L
2)	800	or	200	or	1kg	10L	and	90L
3)	200	or	50	or	250g	1L	and	2L
Australia	250	or	50		250g	1L	or	1L
Canada	200	and	50	and	900g	1.1L	or	1L
Eire 1)	200	or	50	or	250g	1L	and	2L
2)	800	or	200	or	1kg	10L	and	90L
New Zealand	200	or	50	or	250g	1.1L	or	4½L
South Africa	400	and	50	and	250g	1L	and	2L
UK 1)	200	or	50	or	250g	1L	and	2L
2)	800	or	200	or	1kg	10L	and	90L
USA	300	or	75	or	400	1L	or	1L

1) Visitors arriving from EU countries with duty-free items, or from other European countries.
2) Visitors arriving from EU countries with duty paid on items.
3) Residents outside Europe.

Currency restrictions There's no limit on the amount of local or foreign currencies or traveller's cheques that can be brought into or taken out of France, but amounts exceeding 50,000 French francs (or equivalent) must be declared on arrival.

I've nothing to declare.　　**Je n'ai rien à déclarer.**
It's for my own use.　　**C'est pour mon usage personnel.**

DISABLED TRAVELLERS

Paris has not been conceived with the disabled traveller in mind, though things are steadily improving. The Louvre, for instance, suggests special tours designed to ease getting round the museum, and the new TGB library will take into account the needs of the disabled. Airports are now well equipped to help; for Orly south ring (1) 49.75.30.70 and Orly west (1) 46.75.18.18. For Roissy, ring Air Assistance on (1) 48.62.28.24. The RATP (metro and bus network in Paris) offers a *voyage accompagné* service from 9 a.m. to 5 p.m; someone will accompany you during your trip on the RATP. Ring (1) 49.59.96.00 48 hours ahead to book. A similar service can be arranged with the SNCF (train network), by ringing the appropriate railway station. It is worth getting a copy of *Access in Paris*, a guidebook for disabled people; contact Access Project (PHSP), 39 Bradley Gardens, London W13 8HE, UK.

DRIVING IN FRANCE

To take a car into France, you will need:

● A valid driving licence
● Car registration papers
● Insurance coverage (the green card is no longer obligatory but comprehensive coverage is advisory)
● A red warning triangle and a set of spare bulbs

The minimum driving age is 18. Drivers, front- and back-seat passengers are required by law to wear seat belts. Children under the age of 10 may not travel in the front (unless the car has no back seat). Driving on a foreign provisional licence is not permitted in France.

Driving regulations As elsewhere on the continent, drive on the right, overtake on the left and yield right of way to all vehicles coming from the right (except on roundabouts), unless indicated otherwise. In built-up areas, *always* give priority to vehicles coming from the right. In other areas, the more important of the two roads has right of way. The use of car horns in built-up areas is allowed only as a warning. At night, lights should be used for this purpose.

Speed limits On dry roads the speed limit is 130km/h (around 80mph) on toll motorways; 110km/h (70mph) on dual carriageways; 90km/h (55mph) on other country roads; and 45 or 50km/h (30 or 35mph) in built-up areas. *Note*: when roads are wet, all limits are reduced by 10km/h (5mph), except for motorways, where the maximum speed limit in fog, rain or snow is reduced by 20km/h (10mph).

Road conditions Driving in Paris would be an exciting experience – if it weren't for the horrors of parking and some demoralising traffic jams. Thanks to Baron Haussmann, however, and Pompidou's *voie expresse*, numerous broad avenues generally sweep traffic through the capital at a tolerable speed – but you can't rely on it. Ring roads (*périphériques*) round Paris tend to get clogged up at rush hours. Note that motorways (*autoroutes*) outside Paris are expensive. For advance information on traffic conditions, try France-Inter's *Inter-Route* service, which operates 24 hours a day from Paris. Most of the time, English-speaking staff will be there to help you. Phone (1) 48.94.33.33. Then there's the Centre d'Information Autoroutes, 3, rue Edmond Valentin, 75007 Paris, tel. (1) 47.05.90.01.

Parking (*stationnement*). This is a nightmare (as in most capitals), which is why it's better to walk as much as possible.

In the centre most street parking is metered. If you want to leave your car in a *zone bleue* you will need a *disque de stationnement,* a parking disc which you can get from a petrol station, newsagent or stationer. Set it to show the time you arrived and it will indicate when you have to leave; then display it in the car. Look out for the *disque obligatoire* (disc compulsary) sign. Some streets have alternate parking on either side of the street according to which part of the month it is (the dates are marked on the signs).

Breakdowns It's wise to take out an international breakdown insurance before leaving home. Always ask for an estimate before authorizing repairs, and expect to pay TVA (value-added tax) on top of the cost. Two companies which offer 24-hour breakdown service are Automobile Club Secours, tel. (1) 05.05.05.24 (toll-free number) and SOS Dépannage, tel. (1) 47.07.99.99.

Fuel and oil (*essence; huile*). Fuel is available as super (98 octane), normal (90 octane), lead-free (*sans plomb* – usually 98 or *super-green* and sometimes 95 octane) and diesel (*gas-oil*). Note that many garages are shut on Sundays. Avoid buying petrol on motorways, and try to get to a supermarket to fill up – there can be as much as a 15% difference in price.

Fluid measures

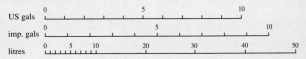

Road signs Most road signs are the standard pictographs used throughout Europe, but you may encounter these written signs as well:

Accotements non stabilisés	Soft shoulders
Chaussée déformée	Uneven road surface
Déviation	Diversion (detour)
Gravillons	Loose gravel
Péage	Toll
Priorité à droite	Yield to traffic from right
Ralentir	Slow down
Serrez à droite/à gauche	Keep right/left
driving licence	**permis de conduire**
car registration papers	**carte grise**
Fill the tank, please.	**Le plein, s'il vous plaît.**
lead-free/three-star/four-star	**sans plomb/normale/super**
My car has broken down.	**Ma voiture est en panne.**
There's been an accident.	**Il y a eu un accident.**

EMERGENCIES (*urgence*)

You can get assistance anywhere in France by dialling 17 for the police (*police secours*); 18 for the fire brigade (*pompiers*), who also turn out for medical emergencies. Paris has an efficient anti-poison centre: tel. 40.37.04.04. You can get advice for other urgent medical problems by calling SOS Médecins on 47.07.77.77 or the SAMU on 45.67.50.50.

Careful!	**Attention!**	Police!	**Police!**
Fire!	**Au feu!**	Stop, thief!	**Au voleur!**
Help!	**Au secours!**		

Can you help me? **Pouvez-vous m'aider?**

ELECTRIC CURRENT

You'll need an adaptor for most British and US plugs for French sockets that have round holes. Although just about everything is 220 volt, you may just occasionally find 110-volt plugs in rural France.

EMBASSIES & CONSULATES

For any major problem, such as loss of passport or all your money, theft, problems with the police or a serious accident, contact your consulate or embassy.

Australia embassy and consulate: 4 Rue Jean-Rey, 75015 Paris; tel. (1) 40.59.33.06; fax (1) 40.59.33.10

Canada embassy: 35 Avenue Montaigne, 75008 Paris; tel. (1) 44.43.29.16; fax (1) 44.43.29.99

Eire embassy: 12 Avenue Foch (enter from 4 Rue Rude), 75016 Paris; tel. (1) 45.00.20.87; fax (1) 45.00.84.17

125

New Zealand	embassy: 7 ter Rue Léonard-de-Vinci, 75116 Paris; tel. (1) 45.00.24.11; fax (1) 45.01.26.39
South Africa	consulate: 59 Quai d'Orsay, 75443 Paris Cedex 07; tel. (1) 45.55.92.37; fax 47.53.99.70
United Kingdom	embassy: 35 Rue du Faubourg-Saint-Honoré, 75008 Paris; tel. (1) 42.66.91.42; consulate: 16, rue d'Anjou, 75008 Paris; tel. (1) 42.66.06.68; fax (1) 40.76.02.87
USA	embassy: 2 Avenue Gabriel, 75008 Paris; tel. (1) 42.96.12.02. Consulate: 2 Rue St Florentin, 75001 Paris (same telephone number); fax (1) 42.66.05.33/42.66.97.83

GETTING THERE

BY AIR
Scheduled flights
Paris is served by two intercontinental airports, Roissy-Charles-de-Gaulle and Orly. Average journey time between Paris and Johannesburg is 14 hours, London 1 hour, New York 7 hours (less than 4 hours by Concorde), Toronto 9 hours.

Charter flights and package tours

From the UK and Eire Most tour operators charter seats on scheduled flights at a reduced price as part of a package deal which could include a weekend or a couple of weeks' stay, a simple bed and breakfast arrangement or a combined 'wine tour' and visit to Paris. Among the inclusive holiday packages are special tours for visitors with a common interest, such as cookery courses, school trips or art.

However, most visitors from the UK travel to France individually, either by booking directly with a ferry operator and taking a car across, or signing up for inclusive holidays which offer fly-drive and touring or self-catering arrangements.

From North America ABC (Advance Booking Charters) provide air passage only (from New York, chicago, Los Angeles and San Francisco to Paris), but OTC (One Stop Inclusive Tour Charter) package deals include airport transfers, hotel, some sightseeing and meals.

Paris is the starting point for many tours of France. Wine tasting, gourmet and cooking tours, as well as tours of the château country are included in package deals leaving from over a dozen major American and Canadian cities, usually on a seasonal basis (April to October) and for periods of from one to three weeks. You can also choose from fly-drive and fly-rail schemes.

From Australia and New Zealand Package deals for Paris are offered by certain airlines. You can also travel by independent arrangement (the usual direct economy flight with unrestricted stopovers) or go on an air-and-car-hire arrangement.

From South Africa There are both excursion fares and numerous package deals including Paris among other European sights.

BY CAR

Cross-channel operators offer plenty of special deals at competitive prices; a good travel agent will help you to find the suitable ferry for your destination. If you like leisurely sea crossings, you might wish to cross to St Malo, Roscoff or Cherbourg; from Calais, the route to Paris is easy and rapid.

BY BUS

Numerous lines serve Paris from regional cities like Bordeaux, Lyons or Nice. Regular services also operate from London to Paris via Calais.

BY RAIL

All the main lines converge on Paris. there is an excellent network of ultra-rapid express trains, TGVs (first and second class, advance booking compulsory, certain trains with supplement). Auto-train services (*Trains Autos Couchettes*) are also available from all major towns.

The journey from London to Paris takes from 6 to 11 hours by train and ferry (depending on the ferry crossing), only 3 hours by train using the Channel Tunnel. British and French railways offer London-to-Paris services with the possibility of sleeper cars from London. From Boulogne hoverport, there's a 2-hour 20-minute turbo-train service to Paris (Gare du Nord).

Tickets Visitors from abroad can buy a *France-Vacances Spécial* pass, valid for specified periods of unlimited travel on first or second class, with reductions on the Paris transport network and one or two days' free car rental (available with first class only), depending on the type of card.

Residents of Europe can purchase an *Inter-Rail* or *Inter-Rail plus* card which allows one month's unlimited second-class travel on most European rail networks. The under-26 Inter-Rail card is also available now for selected zones of Europe (France, Belgium, Luxemburg and Netherlands constitue one zone). The Freedom Pass is available for travel on 3, 5 or 10 days within any month, in one or more of the 26 participating countries of Europe.

People living outside Europe and North Africa can purchase a *Eurailpass* for unlimited rail travel in 16 European countries, including France. This pass must be obtained before leaving home.

LANGUAGE

Even if your French isn't perfect, don't feel inhibited to speak: that's far better as far as the French are concerned than making no effort at all. Never take it for granted that people will speak English.

The Berlitz FRENCH PHRASEBOOK AND DICTIONARY covers almost all situations you're likely to encounter in your travels in France. In addition, the Berlitz French-English/English-French pocket dictionary contains a glossary of 12,500 terms, plus a menu-reader supplement.

Good morning/Good afternoon.	**Bonjour.**
Goodbye.	**Au revoir.**
Thank you.	**Merci.**
Please.	**S'il vous plaît.**
You're welcome.	**Je vous en prie.**
Speak slowly, please.	**Parlez lentement, s'il vous plaît.**

LAUNDRY & DRY CLEANING (*blanchisserie; nettoyage à sec*).

If your hotel will not take care of your laundry or dry cleaning, go to a chain dry cleaners for a quick and cheap service (not recommended, however, for delicate fabrics). There are plenty of laundromats all over Paris, most particularly in the Latin Quarter. A more thorough, careful service inevitably takes longer and is more expensive. Prices vary according to fabric and cut.

When will it be ready?	**Quand est-ce que ce sera prêt?**
I must have it tomorrow morning.	**Il me le faut pour demain matin.**

LOST PROPERTY (*objets trouvés*)

If loss or suspected theft occurs in your hotel, check first at the desk. They may suggest that you report the loss to the local police station (*commissariat*). Restaurant and hotel personnel are quite honest about returning objects left behind; they turn over valuables to the police.

Lost property generally turn up at the Bureau des Objets Trouvés, 36 Rue des Morillons, 75015 Paris. If you've lost a passport, check first with your embassy, as the Bureau des Objets Trouvés would transfer it there. Forms must be filled out in French though there are usually English-speakers on hand.

I've lost my	**J'ai perdu mon**
wallet/handbag/passport	**portefeuille/sac/passeport**

MAPS

Small maps (*plan*) of the city are given away at tourist offices, banks, the big department stores and at hotels. Metro and bus maps are given on request in metro stations. More detailed maps are sold at bookstores and at newstands. A good investment is the pocketable and compact *Plan de Paris* put out by A. Leconte. It contains one large foldout map and small detailed plans of each *arrondissement*, with useful adresses plus a glossary of all street names.

MEDICAL CARE (see also EMERGENCIES)

To put your mind at rest, make sure your health insurance policy covers any illness or accident while on holiday. If you're uncertain, ask your insurance representative, motoring association or travel agent about special holiday insurance plans.

Visitors from EU countries with corresponding health insurance facilities are entitled to medical and hospital treatment under the French social security system. Before leaving home, make sure you find out about the appropriate forms and formalities.

Paris has excellent doctors, surgeons and medical facilities. Most bigger hotels or the consulates have a list of English-speaking doctors and dentists. Doctors who belong to the French social security system (*médecins conventionnés*) charge the minimum.

Two private hospitals serve the Anglo-American community: the American Hospital of Paris, 63, Bd. Victor-Hugo, 92202 Neuilly, tel. (1) 46.41.25.25; and the Hôpital Franco-Britannique, 3 Rue de Barbes, 92300 Levallois-Perret, tel. (1) 46.39.22.22.

Chemist shops (*pharmacies*) are easily identified by the green cross they display. They are helpful in dealing with minor ailments and can recommend a nurse (*infirmière*) if you need injections or other special care. There's always a chemist on night-duty (*service de garde*) and its name and address is displayed in the window of other pharmacies. The Pharmacie des Champs-Elysées, 84 Av. des **130** Champs-Elysées, tel. (1) 45.62.02.41, is open 24 hours a day.

MINITEL

The Minitel has invaded most French homes and public buildings and is on its way to becoming indispensible. It can be used for everything, from ordering a reservation on a TGV train to booking a theatre ticket or looking up someone's telephone number or address (there are no longer telephone directories in telephone cabins). The Minitel most tourists are likely to meet is either in their hotel room or at the post office. A little brochure, *Passeport Tourisme Minitel*, with operating instructions in English (there's nothing very complicated about it) and a list of useful codes is available from tourist offices. Some of the 7,500-plus services are in English.

MONEY MATTERS

Currency The French *franc* (abbreviated F or FF) is divided into 100 *centimes* (ct).

- Coins (*pièces*): 5, 10, 20, 50 centimes; 1, 2, 5, 10, 20 (end 1992) F, FF or sometimes fr.

- Banknotes (*billets*): 20, 50, 100, 200, 500 F.

For currency restrictions, see CUSTOMS & ENTRY FORMALITIES, pp.120–1

Banks and currency exchange offices (*banque; bureaux de change*) see also OPENING HOURS. Always take your passport when you go to change money or traveller's cheques. Your hotel may also come to the rescue, though you'll get a less favourable exchange rate. The same applies to foreign currency or traveller's cheques changed in stores, boutiques, tourist offices or restaurants.

I want to change some pounds/ dollars. **Je voudrais changer des livres sterling/des dollars.**

Credit cards are used in an increasing number of hotels, restaurants, shops and petrol stations, and you can also use them to withdraw cash from any DAB (*distributeurs automatiques de billets*). **131**

Traveller's cheques and Eurocheques are widely accepted throughout France. Outside Paris, it's still preferable to have some ready cash with you.

Sales tax A value-added tax (TVA) is imposed on almost all goods and services, and is usually included in the price. In hotels and restaurants, this is on top of a service charge.

Visitors from non-EC countries will be refunded the TVA on their larger purchases. Ask the sales assistant for the appropriate form, to be filled out and handed to French customs on departure.

Do you accept traveller's cheques/this credit card?

Acceptez-vous les chèques de voyage/cette carte de crédit?

MUSEUM & MONUMENT PASS
The *Carte Musées et Monuments*

Grants unlimited access to no less than 63 museums and monuments in Paris and the area, running from the Musée des Egouts (Drains Museum) to the Louvre and the Château de Versailles. The pass is valid for one, three or five days and can be bought from tourist offices, metro stations, museum or monument ticket offices.

NEWSPAPERS & MAGAZINES (*journal; revue/magazine*)

As befits a cosmopolitan city, there is a very wide range of dailies, weeklies and monthlies in English and other languages, quite apart from the French press. You'll find them in kiosks and *maisons de la Presse*. Most of them arrive on the newstands on the day of publication. The Paris edition of the *International Herald Tribune* is available at most newsagents. *Pariscope* and *L'Officiel des Spectacles* are the best known weeklies on what's on in Paris. A very helpful companion to this guide is the Berlitz Paris Address Book, where over 1,000 addresses and commentaries cover absolutely all sides of Parisian life.

OPENING HOURS (heures d'ouverture)

Avoid using lunch hours for 'administrative' task: the long-drawn-out Parisian lunch is becoming a distant memory, but businesses and smaller shops close for an hour or so, between 12 and 2.30 p.m.

Banks tend to open from 9 a.m. to 5 p.m. on weekdays (many closing for lunch from 12 till 2) and close either on Saturdays or Mondays. All banks close on major national or regional holidays and most close early on the day preceding a public holiday.

Main post offices are open from 8 a.m. to 7 p.m. on weekdays and from 8 a.m. till noon on Saturdays. Smaller post offices close for lunch from 12 till 2 or 2.30 p.m., and close at 5 or 6 p.m.

Grocers, bakeries, tobacconists, food shops are open from 7 a.m. to 7 p.m.(or later, sometimes up to midnight), Monday to Saturday. Food shops are often open on Sunday morning. Small shops usually shut at lunchtime, from 12.30 to 2 p.m.

Other shops, department stores, boutiques, galleries are open from 8 or generally 9 or 9.30 a.m. to 6.30 or 7 p.m. (sometimes later in summer), Tuesday to Saturday, and are closed Monday morning or all day Monday.

Museums, monuments are open from 10 a.m. to 5 or 5.30 p.m. (variable). Closing day tends to be Tuesday (*except* for the Musée d'Orsay – beware of queues!). It's best to check before going.

P

PLANNING YOUR BUDGET

The following prices in French francs (F) should give you an idea of the cost of living in the French capital. However, they must be regarded as approximate and taken as broad guidelines; inflation in France, as elsewhere, rises steadily.

Airport transfer Bus to Orly 23 F, to Charles-de-Gaulle 48 F. train (second class) to Orly 22 F, to Charles-de-Gaulle 27.50 F. Taxi to Orly approx. 170 F, to Charles-de-Gaulle approx. 220 F.

Bicycle hire 44/55 F per day, plus 1,000 F refundable deposit.

Car hire (international company). Renault 5: 276.34 F per day, 4.40 F per km, 1,925 F per week with unlimited mileage. Renault 19: 343.94 F per day, 5.05 F per km, 2,550 F per week with unlimited mileage. Renault Safrane: 513.54 per day, 6.88 F per km, 4,300 F per week with unlimited mileage. Mercedes 190: 859,85 F per day; 8.92 F per km; 6,500 F per week with unlimited mileage. Tax and insurance included.

Cigarettes French 10–13 F; foreign 15–20 F, cigars 30–60 F each.

Entertainment Discothèque (admission and first drink) 80–150F; nightclub with dinner and floor show 300–650 F; cinema 40–50 F. Special rates for students/groups/Wednesdays 26–35 F.

Guides 640–830 F for a half-day.

Hotels (double room with bath). ****L 1,200–2,500 F; **** 900–1,500 F; *** 500–800 F; ** 350–500 F; * 180–350 F.

Meals and drinks Continental breakfast, hotel 50–150 F; café 30–60 F. Lunch or dinner (in a fairly good establishment) 150–350 F, coffee 8–12 F, beer 15–40 F, bottle of wine 90 F and up, cocktail 50–90 F, whisky 55 F, cognac 40–60 F.

Metro Ticket 7 F; 10 tickets (*carnet*) 41 F; weekly *coupon jaune* (*hebdomadaire*) bought for each Monday to Sunday only (valid on buses and metro) 63 F; monthly *carte orange* 219 F (also valid on buses). 'Paris Visite' ticket (bus or metro) 65F for two days, 90 F for three days, 145 F for five days.

Sightseeing Boats: adults 40 F, children 20 F; museums 20–35 F. *Carte Musées* 60F for one day, 120F for three, 170F for five days.

Taxis start at 12 F (an extra 5 F is charged at train stations and air terminals), 3.23 F per kilometre. Night rates are higher.

POLICE

The blue-uniformed *police municipale* (or *gardiens de la paix*, peace-keepers, as they are more poetically known) are as a general rule most courteous and helpful to tourists – though one cannot count on their indulgence on parking or speeding matters. They keep law and order, direct traffic and hem in demonstrations.

The CRS (*compagnies républicaines de Sécurité*) are the 'fierce' ones, wielding batons and shields and quelling demonstrations that have got out of hand. The elegantly dressed *Garde républicaine*, often on horseback and accompanied by a very good band, turn out for ceremonies and parades. Outside Paris and the main cities are the *gendarmes*; they wear blue trousers and black jackets with white belts and are responsible for traffic and crime investigation.

If you need to call for police help, dial 17 in Paris and all over France.

Where's the nearest police station? **Où est le commissariat de police le plus proche?**

POST OFFICE (*poste*)

French post offices display a sign with a stylized blue bird and/or the words 'Postes et Télécommunications', 'P&T' or nowadays simply 'La Poste'. They are usually open from 8 a.m. to 7 p.m. Monday to Friday and from 8 a.m. to noon on Saturday. The post office at 52 Rue du Louvre is open 24 hours a day, every day. Queues can be quite long. The post office at 71, Avenue des Champs-Elysée is open on Sundays and public holidays from 10 a.m. to 12 p.m. and 2 p.m to 8.p.m., and until 10p.m. on weekdays.

In addition to normal mail service, you can make local or long-distance phone calls from post offices, buy stamps and *télécartes* (phone cards), send telegrams and faxes, and receive or send money at any counter.

Letters may be delivered within hours in the Paris district by sending them *postexpress* from the post office. Another quick and even cheaper system for delivering a message is the *message téléphoné;* tel. 3655.

N.B. While you *can* theoretically always buy stamps (*timbres*) at tobacconists and occasionally at hotels or from postcard vendors or souvenir shops, the sales people are disinclined to sell stamps unless you purchase something else. You can, however, buy *télécartes* there (see TELEPHONES).

Mail (*courrier*). If you don't know ahead of time where you'll be staying, you can have your mail addressed to you *poste restante* (general delivery) c/o Poste restante, 52 Rue du Louvre, 75001 Paris. This is Paris's main post office, open 24 hours a day, every day. You can collect it for a small fee on presentation of your passport. American Express, at 11 Rue Scribe, 75009 Paris, performs the same service. Post can be sluggish in the summer months.

PUBLIC HOLIDAYS (*jour férié*)

Public offices, banks and most shops close on public holidays, though you'll find the odd corner shop open. If one of these days falls on a Tuesday or Thursday, many French people take the Monday or Friday off as well for a long weekend (this doesn't usually curtail activity in shops or businesses, however).

January	*Jour de l'An*	New Year's Day
1 May	*Fête du Travail*	Labour Day
8 May	*Fête de la Victoire*	Victory Day (1945)
14 July	*Fête nationale*	Bastille Day
15 August	*Assomption*	Assumption
1 November	*Toussaint*	All Saints' Day
11 November	*Armistice*	Armistice Day (1918)
25 December	*Noël*	Christmas Day
Movable dates:	*Lundi de Pâques*	Easter Monday
	Ascension	Ascension
	Lundi de Pentecôte	Whit Monday

Are you open tomorrow?	**Est-ce que vous ouvrez demain?**

PUBLIC TRANSPORT

Bus (*autobus*). Bus transport round Paris is efficient though not always fast. Stops are marked by red and yellow signs, with bus numbers posted, and you'll find bus itineraries under bus shelters. Most buses run from 7 a.m. to 8.30 p.m., some till 12.30 p.m. Service is reduced on Sundays and public holidays. Special buses for night-owls, the 'Noctambus', run along ten main routes serving the capital, from 1.30 a.m. to 5.30 a.m. every hour, with Châtelet as the hub. (Ask for a plan at any metro station.)

Bus journeys may take up one, two or three tickets, depending on the distance. You can buy a ticket as you board the bus, but if you use public transport a lot, it's cheaper to buy a book of tickets (*carnet*), from any metro station. (Bus and metro tickets are inter-changeable.) You can also look into purchasing special one-, three- or five-day tourist passes or the *carte orange* (see METRO, see below).

A simple and excellent way to sightsee is to hop on and off, wherever you like and as often as you like, one of the coaches (*cars*) of the Inter-Transport or the double-decker Parisbus – all on the same ticket. The route followed in a $1^1/2$ to $2^1/2$-hour tour (departure every hour) takes in the most interesting highlights of Paris (Palais de Chaillot, Etoile, Eiffel Tower, Louvre, Madeleine, Montparnasse, etc). Tickets are available at bus stops or from Les Coches parisiens, 9 Place de la Madeleine.

The Bat-O-bus is a summer river bus, with five stops between the Eiffel Tower and the Hôtel-de-Ville (see p.117).

Metro Paris's metro is possibly one of the most efficient, fastest, cleanest and convenient underground railway systems in existence today. It's also one of the cheapest, and it keeps growing to suit passengers' needs. Express lines (RER) get you into the centre of Paris from distant suburbs in about 15 minutes, with a few stops in between.

If you use the metro regularly, it's worth investing in a *carnet* (book) of tickets that is also valid for the bus network. A metro ticket also does the trick with the RER, provided that you stay within Paris and don't go to the suburbs.

For longer stays, a *coupon jaune* (valid for a week) and a *carte orange* (valid for a month) are well worth it. They can be used on buses and the metro. (You'll need a passport photo for the carte orange.) There is also a special tourist ticket called *Paris Visite*, valid for three or five days, allowing unlimited travel on bus or first-class metro and a day ticket, *Formule 1*, valid for the metro, RER, buses, suburban trains and the Montmartre funicular.

Metro stations have big, easy-to-read maps. The system is easy to pick up. The service starts at 5.30 a.m. and finishes round 1 a.m.

As just about everywhere else, it is not recommended to travel alone after about 10.30 p.m. The RATP has an information office at 53 ter Quai des Grands Augustins, 75271 Paris, Cedex 6. You can call them round the clock on (1) 43.46.14.14.

Trains (*train*). The SNCF (French Railways Authority) runs fast, punctual and comfortable trains on an efficient network. The high-speed services (TGV – *train à grande vitesse*) operating on selected routes are excellent, but more expensive than the average train. Seat reservation on TGVs is compulsory, and you have to pay for it.

The main stations in Paris are the Gare du Nord (for British connections), Gare de l'Est, Gare d'Austerlitz, Gare Saint-Lazare, Gare Montparnasse and Gare de Lyon (for links to the Riviera, Switzerland and Italy). Various categories of ticket are available. Make sure you get your ticket punched *before* getting on board, by inserting it in one of the orange machines (called *machines à composter* or *composteur*) on the way to the platform. If it is not clipped and dated, the ticket collector is entitled to fine you on the train.

TAXIS

Inexpensive and rapid, taxis are a bargain, though there'll be extras for putting luggage in the boot and for getting picked up at a station or airport. Also, taxis cannot by law carry more than three passengers. You'll come across taxis cruising around, or at stands all over town. Ask for a receipt if you need it (*une fiche*). There are three different rates, according to the zones covered or the time of the day (you'll be charged more between 7 p.m. and 7 a.m. the following day and on Sundays). An average fare between Roissy Airport and Paris centre might be 220 FF in the daytime, 280 FF at night. If you have any problems with a driver, you can register a complaint with the Service des Taxis, 36 Rue des Morillons, 75732 Paris; tel. (1) 45.31.14.80.

TELEPHONE (téléphone)

Long-distance and international calls can be made from any phone box, but if you need assistance in placing the call, you may be happier doing so from the post office or your hotel (where you'll probably pay a supplement).

The system is both efficient and simple, with the only problem that just about all Parisian phone boxes only take télécartes of 50 or 120 units. You can buy them at post offices or tobacconists. Coin-operated phones guzzle up 50-centime, 1-franc, 2-franc and 5-franc coins.

To make an international call, dial 19 and wait for a continuous burring tone before dialling the rest of the number. Here are the full codes for the main English-speaking countries:

Australia	19…61	**South Africa**	19…27
Canada	19… 1	**UK**	19…44
Eire	19…35	**USA**	19… 1
New Zealand	19…64		

For international inquiries, add 33 between 19 and the code of your chosen country, e.g. 19 33 44 (inquiries for the UK). For inquiries on US or Canadian numbers, dial 11 instead of 1, eg. 19 33 11).

For long-distance calls within France, there are no area codes (just dial the 8-digit number of the person you want to call), *except* when telephoning from Paris or its suburb (Ile-de-France) to the provinces (dial 16 and wait for the dialling tone, then dial the 8-digit number of the subscriber). From the provinces to Paris or the Ile-de-France (dial 16, wait for the dialling tone, then dial 1 followed by the 8-digit number). If all else fails, call the operator for help (12).

TIME DIFFERENCES

France keeps to Central European Time (GMT+1). Summer time (GMT+2) comes into force from late March to end September. The days are long at the height of summer, when it's still light at 11 p.m.

New York	London	**Paris**	Sydney	Auckland
6 a.m.	11 a.m.	**noon**	8 p.m.	10 p.m.

What time is it? **Quelle heure est-il?**

TIPPING

A little tip can go a long way in Paris. Generally, a tip has been included in the restaurant bill and, increasingly, tips are being given only for a particularly appreciated service – except for museum guides. If the prices aren't inclusive (*service non compris, service en sus*), you can add up to 10 per cent to your bill:

Hotel porter, per bag	5 F
Hotel maid, per week	50–100 F
Lavatory attendant	4 F
Waiter	5–10% (optional)
Taxi driver	10–15%
Tour guide	10%

TOURIST INFORMATION OFFICES (*office de tourisme*)

Before going to Paris you can obtain a great deal of up-to-date information from the French national tourist office in your country. On the spot, you'll find the French tourist office at 127 Avenue des Champs-Elysées, 75008 Paris; tel. (1) 49.52.53.54; fax (1) 49.52.53.00. Staff will be able to help you with anything, from information to booking accommodation and the office is open from 9 a.m. to 8 p.m. Currency exchange can be handled there as well as across the street. Other branches are located in major stations, airports and terminals.

To get a selection of the principal weekly events in English, call (1) 49.52.53.55. For information on the *départements* surrounding Paris, you can contact the CRT Ile de France, 26, Avenue de l'Opéra, 75015 Paris; tel.(1) 42.60.28.62. To know more about what's happening at Disneyland Paris resort, ring (1) 64.74.30.00.

There are French National Tourist Offices in the following English-speaking countries:

Australia	Kindersley House, 33 Bligh Street, Sydney, NSW 2000; tel. (2) 231 5244
Canada	1981 Avenue McGill College, Suite 490, Esso Tower, Montreal, Que. H3 A2 W9; tel. (514) 288 4264
	1, Dundas Street West, Suite 2405, Box 8, Toronto, Ont. M5 G1 Z3; tel. (416) 593 4717
South Africa	Carlton Centre, 10th Floor, P.O. Box 1081, Johannesburg 2000; tel. (11) 331 9252
UK	178 Piccadilly, London W1V 0AL; tel. (01891) 244 123; fax (071) 493 6594
USA	610 Fifth Avenue, New York, NY 10020; tel. (212) 757 1125
	645 North Michigan Avenue, Suite 630, Chicago, Illinois 60611; tel. (312) 337 6301
	9401 Wilshire Boulevard, Beverly Hills, California 90212; tel. (213) 272 2661
	1 Hallidie Plaza, San Francisco, California 94102; tel. (415) 986 4174
	World Trade Center, N103, 2050 Stemmons Freeway, P.O. Box 58610, Dallas, Texas 75258; tel. (214) 742 7011

Y

YOUTH HOSTELS (auberges de Jeunesse)

For more information, ask for the free guide to all French Youth Hostels, obtainable from the Fédération Unie des Auberges de Jeunesse (FUAJ), 27 Rue Pagol, 75018 Paris; tel. (1) 44.89.87.27. Those in Paris are stretched to capacity all year round, so booking first is essential.

Index

Where there is more than one set of references, the one in **bold** refers to the main entry.

143

Berlitz – pack the world in your pocket!

Africa
Algeria
Kenya
Morocco
South Africa
Tunisia

Asia, Middle East
China
Egypt
Hong Kong
India
Indonesia
Japan
Jerusalem
Malaysia
Singapore
Sri Lanka
Taiwan
Thailand

Australasia
Australia
New Zealand
Sydney

Austria, Switzerland
Austrian Tyrol
Switzerland
Vienna

Belgium, The Netherlands
Amsterdam
Brussels

British Isles
Channel Islands
Dublin
Ireland
London
Scotland

Caribbean, Latin America
Bahamas
Bermuda
Cancún and Cozumel
Caribbean
French West Indies
Jamaica
Mexico

Mexico City/Acapulco
Puerto Rico
Rio de Janeiro
Southern Caribbean
Virgin Islands

Central and Eastern Europe
Budapest
Hungary
Moscow and St Petersburg
Prague

France
Brittany
Châteaux of the Loire
Côte d'Azur
Dordogne
Euro Disney Resort
France
Normandy
Paris
Provence

Germany
Berlin
Munich
Rhine Valley

Greece, Cyprus and Turkey
Athens
Corfu
Crete
Cyprus
Greek Islands
Istanbul
Rhodes
Turkey

Italy and Malta
Florence
Italy
Malta
Milan and the Lakes
Naples
Rome
Sicily
Venice

North America
Alaska Cruise Guide
Boston

California
Canada
Disneyland and the Theme Parks of Southern California
Florida
Greater Miami
Hawaii
Los Angeles
Montreal
New Orleans
New York
San Francisco
Toronto
USA
Walt Disney World and Orlando
Washington

Portugal
Algarve
Lisbon
Madeira

Scandinavia
Copenhagen
Helsinki
Oslo and Bergen
Stockholm
Sweden

Spain
Barcelona
Canary Islands
Costa Blanca
Costa Brava
Costa del Sol
Costa Dorada and Barcelona
Costa Dorada and Tarragona
Ibiza and Formentera
Madrid
Mallorca and Menorca
Seville

IN PREPARATION
Bali and Lombok
Edinburgh
Israel